The Vance Havner Quotebook

The Vance Havner Quotebook

**Sparkling Gems from
the Most Quoted Preacher
in America**

Compiled by
Dennis J. Hester

BAKER BOOK HOUSE
Grand Rapids, Michigan 49506

Contents

Contents

Contents

Contents

Contents

Foreword

No one can turn a phrase any better than Vance Havner. From both pulpit and pen he has sprinkled penetrating truths throughout his down-to-earth, Bible-centered messages, leaving his listeners laughing and enlightened and convicted. Whether preaching from humble brush arbors or auditoriums on the boulevard, he speaks — to use his own words — to comfort the afflicted and to afflict the comfortable.

Havner is a wordsmith. With as little formal education as he's had, one wonders how he has come to use words so clearly and cleverly. He gives the phrase "play on words" new meaning. (For example, in his devotional book, *Pepper 'n' Salt*, Havner writes, "If the creation story, the virgin birth, and the resurrection are only myths, then I'm myth-taken and myth-ified and mytherable.")

Unembarrassed by homiletic professors, Havner

arouses — and holds — one's attention with his home-spun humor while the Holy Spirit stimulates and penetrates the soul with the convicting message of God.

"I use humor, but not to entertain," says Havner, a natural humorist. But what else can we expect from an antique of a fellow, a fool for Christ, a foreigner to modernity who has experienced everything from fishing in creeks to flying in jets?

One of Havner's favorite stories is one he likes to tell on himself. It seems that when he went to preach a trial sermon at a Baptist church in Charleston, South Carolina, many years ago, he preached on the subject of hypocrites. One of the deacons was heard to respond, "Well, he's not looking for work." (Havner ended up serving for five years at the church.)

Havner's ability to communicate lies in his uniqueness. "Be different," he advises. "Don't be odd or peculiar just to be different, but be yourself. You never know when God will use that different angle, way of speaking or writing to touch someone in a new way."

Why have ministers from all over the country quoted Havner's one-liners and peppered their sermons with his illustrations? Why has Havner turned down more invitations in his later years than three full-time evangelists could commit themselves to? Probably because he has a fresh word from God, uncontaminated with the desire for fame or fortune. The heart of Havner's ministry has always been revival and the center of his message has always been Jesus Christ. Jesus has been Havner's first love, his Rock, his Message and Master for seventy years. He stands in the shadow of Christ's cross that his Lord may shine. On every occasion, to the best of Havner's ability, he has lifted up the name of Jesus.

As one listens to Havner preach or reads the account of his life in *Threescore and Ten* (or his biography, *Journey from Jugtown,* by Douglas M. White), one is quickly convinced that here is one who did it his way—or better still, God's way.

While Havner's greatest teacher has been the Lord and his Word, he has also benefitted from the wise counsel of other Christians, who have inspired him intellectually as well as spiritually. He recalls an incident that took place long ago at a time when, as a young preacher, he was trying to find his way.

"I'll never forget meeting R. A. Torrey while riding on a train. He asked me what I was doing. I told him I was interested in a little of this and a little of that. He looked at me with those steel-gray eyes of his and said sternly, 'Young man, pick one thing and stick to it.'

"I never forgot those words. I still believe God would have us sharp as a spear, pointing in one direction instead of like a broom pointing in all directions."

For Havner, social functions are not something he cherishes. "I would gladly exchange them all for a walk in the woods at eventide to hear a wood thrush sing," he says. "It's difficult to find a place to walk and meditate on the things of God today. You may get run over by one of these joggers. You can't meditate gasping for breath. Recently I heard about a man who died of a heart attack jogging from a health food store. I'm always calling preachers to more meditation, reflection, and solitude within this rat race we live in. If we do not 'come apart' to be with the Lord, we will surely 'come apart'."

Not many soul winners have the ability to preach tough and tender like Havner. Even though he speaks prophetically, he tempers his message with pastoral care.

With compassion he spoke to a senior citizens group in his home church, First Baptist of Greensboro, North Carolina. "You folks don't need a sermon," he said. "You need an encouraging word from one who's been on the road for a long time." Then, before the elderly folks could consider complacency, Havner charged them with a challenge. "We are serving the Lord of the leftovers. Jesus said go get the leftovers — the scraps — from the feeding of the five thousand. Some of you folks have some more time left. You have experiences, money, and talent. What are you doing with it? Don't waste it; use it for God. Old Caleb was eighty-five when he asked God for a mountain. He wanted to keep going and growing for the Lord.

God help us to give a good account in these last years of our lives."

Truly a preacher's best friend, Havner encourages speakers of the Word to be writers as well. "If I could only get preachers to realize that what they write, if it's good, will last longer than they will. . . . You never know when the Spirit may breathe on some troubled soul or discouraged servant and begin a blaze that may sweep beyond their wildest imagination. It's a shame those who can write, won't."

Havner's love and support especially abound for "young Timothys" and all Christians "who mean business for God." He started a scholarship fund for students serious about their education and about serving God. So far, the fund has helped more than 250 students from all over the country.* "There isn't a day goes by that I don't receive a letter of thanks from one of those students," Havner says.

There is no way this side of heaven to estimate the eternal good and undying challenge Havner's prophetic messages have brought to ministers and churches across the country. He has faithfully honored God by courageously speaking to our age, convicting our hearts, revealing our sins, and pointing to Jesus as the only remedy.

Today, much of Vance Havner's time is spent in

*The Vance Havner Scholarship Fund, Inc., P.O. Box 1048, Greensboro, North Carolina 27402.

reflecting about the things of God instead of traveling and preaching. He still has a heart for revival and an encouraging word for fellow ministers who stop by to visit him at Friends Home in Greensboro, North Carolina.

Dennis J. Hester

Acknowledgments

To research and compile hundreds of Havner's timely quotes has been a labor of love. I appreciate the people at Baker Book House for believing in this project as I have and giving me the chance to see it become a reality.

I also wish to thank Dick Stevens of Steven's Book Shop in Wake Forest, North Carolina, who helped me secure many of Havner's out-of-print books.

Many thanks to my dear friend Karen Joiner who has encouraged me throughout this project and has been a helpful editor and typist.

Thanks also to Martha Barnes, who lightened my burden of typing the final draft of this manuscript.

Most of all thanks to Vance Havner for his priceless friendship and encouragement to me as a preacher and writer.

I pray this compilation of Havner's quotes will provide moments of delightful browsing as well as a stimulating resource for ministers and laymen alike who seek to communicate the gospel.

Dennis J. Hester

The Vance Havner Quotebook

Abraham	America
Abundance	Ancestors
Abundant living	Anointing
Adultery	Apostle Paul
Adversaries	Appearance
Advice	Atheist
Age	Average
Alcoholism	Awakening
Alive	

Abraham

Abraham's tent knew no secure foundations, only pegs driven in the desert sand. The gates of God's city are open to those who do His commandments (Rev. 22:14).

Abraham did not know where he was going immediately, but he knew where he was going ultimately. He did not know the Whither but he knew the Whom. He believed God, and, being sure of his destiny, he did not worry about his destination.

Abundance

We have never had more to live on and less to live for.

Abundant living

The church is not a nursery for babies still on milk who should long since have been on meat. Sometimes the church does become a spiritual hospital for some who need examination, diagnosis and treatment, even surgery. And it does partake of the function of a nursery to young Christians. But we must get over the idea that it is normal to be weak and sickly when we should be living abundantly.

4

Adultery

We recognize adultery in the slums, but not in Hollywood. Illegitimacy has become respectable and is subsidized by the welfare state.

Adversaries

It's time we stopped groaning over our adversaries and started glorying in our allies. The battle is the Lord's. The victory is already won. Our Waterloo is behind us.

Advice

If I were giving advice to any young preacher— or to any Christian, for that matter—I would say, don't expect too much and don't expect too little.

Age

We need youth to keep things from going too slow and age to keep things from going too fast. And between the two, the "over-forties" have the supreme opportunity of balancing enthusiasm with experience.

We have always needed old people to keep things from going too fast and young people to keep them from going too slow. Youth has fire and age has light and we need both.

We honor God by asking for great things when they are part of His promise. We dishonor Him and cheat ourselves when we ask for molehills where He has offered mountains. Let not advancing years cause you to settle for less than His best. Why shouldn't His warrior's last victory be his greatest? His old soldiers never die and they need not just fade away.

Alcoholism

Total abstinence is considered Victorian and puritanical. We discuss what to do about alcoholism, but nobody seems to want to do much about alcohol. And that is simply a matter of trying to mop up the floor while you leave the faucet running.

Alive

Our Lord says that He is the One "which was dead and is alive." He is not the One who was alive and is dead! That is true of Mohammed and Buddha and every other religious teacher; but our Lord is not in that category for His tomb is empty.

America

If America is not buried by Red Russia from without, we may be smothered by Red Tape from within.

America is fractured and fragmented into hundreds of little groups wanting their own rights while nobody seems to care what happens to the country. A house divided against itself cannot stand.

At the rate America is decaying morally, we shall have to change our national symbol from an eagle to a vulture.

America is laughing itself to death in a vain attempt to drown its sorrows and forget its fears. Behind a thin veneer of hilarity, there are more broken homes, hearts, minds, and lives than ever in our history.

We're so smart in America we can walk on the moon, but it's not safe to walk in the park.

Too many people within our borders are Americans only in name but un-American in their hearts and anti-American in their conduct.

I am thankful that I came along at the turn of the century in time to enjoy a few of the Good Years before 1914 when World War I turned America in another direction—from which she has never returned. We changed gears then. We started a new tune in a different key.

America is not a Christian nation. There is only one Christian nation — God's people, the church of Jesus Christ.

Today America is spiritually sick, starving in the midst of abundance, a nation of paupers in a land of plenty.

America will improve when we have better Americans and the church will improve when we have better Christians.

We Americans have become used to the Gospel. Familiarity has bred complacency, if not contempt.

Ancestors

Ancestry is a fascinating study but the best part, as with potatoes, is usually under the ground. Investigating the family tree is risky business and can be embarrassing.

Anointing

Without the anointing of the Holy Spirit the preacher may storm, the teacher may strive, the Christian worker may sweat, but all to no avail.

Apostle Paul

I can hear some of Paul's old friends saying: "Too bad about Saul of Tarsus. He got off to a good start. He was a brilliant student of Gamaliel. But one day on the road to Damascus he had something like a sunstroke and he has been a religious fanatic ever since. Stays in jail a lot of the time and, as soon as he gets out, gets into trouble and back he goes. What a tragic failure!" We have forgotten Paul's contemporaries, however, and are still reading Paul.

Paul did not say, "To me to live is Christ first." With Paul, Christ was First and Last, Beginning and Ending, Author and Finisher. He was Alpha and Omega—and all the alphabet between.

Paul was in Nero's prison, but he was not Nero's prisoner. He was the prisoner of Jesus Christ.

It has been said that Paul had only two days on his calendar. He who is ready for today is ready for that day and he who is ready for that day is ready for today.

Appearance

One does not have to be a psychiatrist to read marks of vicious temper, hidden resentment, evil thoughts. They show in the droop of the mouth, the wrinkled forehead, the glint in the eye. Abraham Lincoln once objected to a certain appointment because he did not like the candidate's face. Someone interposed, "But Mr. President, a man cannot help how he looks." Mr. Lincoln replied: "He can't help how he looks when he comes into this world but he can help how he looks after forty years."

Atheist

An atheist has a sign on the wall of his office that read, "God Is Nowhere." A little girl saw it and exclaimed, "Look! It says, 'God Is Now Here!'"

Average

Normal does not mean average. Average run-of-the-mill Christianity is our main problem. We have confused luke-warmness with the norm. The vast majority of Sunday-morning parishioners take pride in being middle-of-the-roaders. The New Testament Christian lives above the average.

Awakening

In this day of anarchy, apostasy and apathy, we face three possibilities. The return of our Lord is a certainty and His coming again may be imminent. If He tarry, the Judgment of God may fall upon our unrepentant land. The third possibility is a spiritual awakening, a heavenly visitation in revival among God's people.

Baptism

Basics

Being and doing

Belief

Bible

Bigness

Blessing

Blueprints

Bondage

Bread

Broken things

Burdens

Baptism

We may never be martyrs but we can die to self, to sin, to the world, to our plans and ambitions. That is the significance of baptism; we died with Christ and rose to a new life.

13

Basics

In a day when the living faith of the dead has become the dead faith of the living, just as America needs to get back to the Constitution, so the church needs to return to the cross and the Bible.

Being and doing

This is a day when we are so busy doing everything that we have no time to be anything. Even religiously we are so occupied with activities that we have no time to know God.

Belief

I think of the preacher who attended an old-fashioned camp meeting and "got happy." He shouted his tongue out and his collar down. Next day a friend said, "You don't feel today like you did yesterday." "No," he answered, "but I believe today like I did yesterday."

14

We must not only believe God, we must believe we believe God. Like the silly habit of going back to see if you really did lock that door, an unsettled state of spiritual indecision is developed by doubting souls. They never "close the gate" behind them, they are forever reconsidering their decisions. They are never sure of their conversion or their consecration.

It is appalling how little our church members know of what they are supposed to believe. Some do not know what they are supposed to believe. Some do not know what they believe and many do not practice what they believe.

Unless we can recover the original meaning of faith in Christ and get a new crop of real believers we are going to have a church as different from the first church as head belief is different from heart trust.

Thomas wanted to see and touch, the evidence of the senses, and so wanted a smaller blessing than he already had in believing without seeing.

15

Believing God is not religious auto-suggestion. It is not the flesh engaged in positive thinking. It is the Christian, the one in whom Christ lives, taking God at His Word.

You can't preach it like it is if you don't belive it like it was.

Bible

We must live in the Book. But it is equally necessary, if such results are to be secured, that the Book live in us. "Thou hast words of eternal life," said Peter to the Master.

More Bibles are bought and fewer read than any other book.

It is always easier to understand what the Bible says than to understand what somebody thinks it meant to say.

I am certain that the Bible is the Word of God. Either it is or it isn't, and either all of it is the Word of God or we never can be sure of any of it. It is either absolute or obsolete. If we have to start changing this verse, toning down that, apologizing for this and making allowances for that, we might as well give up, so we must take it as it is or leave it alone.

If you see a Bible that is falling apart, it probably belongs to someone who isn't!

Speed-reading may be a good thing but it was never meant for the Bible. It takes calm, thoughtful, prayerful meditation on the Word to extract its deepest nourishment.

The Bible humbles or hardens the human heart. "He that believeth on him is not condemned: but he that believeth not is condemned already . . ." (John 3:18). If we hear it and do not do what it says, we deceive ourselves. It is not like Homer or Shakespeare. We do not go away the same after we have heard the Word of God. We have to do something about its message, for we cannot leave it alone. We may think we have done nothing about it, but it will do something to us.

17

Bigness

The itch for bigness is a dangerous thing. It has made a castaway of many a man whom God once richly blessed. A man should desire to be neither larger nor smaller than pleases God. Better than that, he should not bother at all about how large or how small but rather how faithful he shall be.

Blessing

We can never be blessed until we learn that we can bring nothing to Christ but our need.

Blueprints

We draw up a design of what we want to do and be and show it to God for His blessings. We do not first inquire, "Lord, what wilt Thou have me to do?" We make a show of seeking His favor but it is His stamp upon our blueprints that we are after.

Bondage

The preacher who is concerned with gaining a reputation, rising in his profession, is always in bondage. Every great opportunity finds him tense and nervous for fear he will not "put it over." He measures success by audience response, the compliments of his hearers, his rating among his contemporaries.

Bread

I saw on a church bulletin board these words: "Religion is bread for daily use, not cake for special occasions." Too often the grace of God is cake, not bread. Our experience of God in Christ is thought of as something special for Sundays and emergencies and unusual religious occasions. The Spirit-filled life, the deeper life, the victorious life — call it what you will — is thought of as something extra, irregular, occasional, now and then, instead of the normal experience of every Christian.

19

Broken things

God uses broken things: broken soil and broken clouds to produce grain; broken grain to produce bread; broken bread to feed our bodies. He wants our stubbornness broken into humble obedience.

Burdens

When a pedestrian with a heavy load is picked up by a motorist, he puts his burden down in the car; he does not keep it on his shoulder. The God who can carry you can carry your load. So cast all your care upon Him for He careth for you.

C

Called

Catacombs

Change

Character

Chastisement

Children

Choices

Christ

Christian

Christianity

Christian life

Christians

Christmas

Church

Citizens of heaven

Civilization

Classification

Comfort

Comforter

Commandments

Committees

Communism

Companionship

Compassion

Complacency

Complaining

Compromise

Conversion

Conviction

Country people

Country preachers and
  churches

Creation

Criminals

Criticism

Cross

Crucifixion

Cry

Cults

Curiosity

Called

Never mind whether or not the mission will be a success. Isaiah was told that his hearers would not receive his message. We are not called to succeed, we are called to go. And when we go He goes along!

Catacombs

Today much of the professing church has gone in for theatrics, running a showboat instead of a lifeboat, staging a performance instead of living an experience, a "form of godliness without the power thereof." We are playing to the grandstand of a pagan age. What a different "show" from the apostles and the early Christians dying for Christ before howling throngs in the Colosseum! We are not sufferers in the arena; we are spectators in the grandstand. We have come a long way from the Catacombs!

Change

There is no sense in getting into a dither just because we have split the atom and are photographing Mars. The Bible is still God's Word and Jesus Christ is the same yesterday, today, and forever. Nothing important has changed.

We cannot change our hearts, but we can change our minds; and when we change our minds, God will change our hearts. "He that believeth on him is not condemned; but he that believeth not is condemned already, because he hath not believed in the name of the only begotten Son of God" (John 3:18).

Character

We may speed up our travel and our reading these days, but not experience. It must be seasoned and there is no way to grow a saint overnight. Speed reading was never meant for Bible study, and character, like the oak, does not spring up like a mushroom.

Today the quality of our church people is at a
frightening low. We are many but not much. Doing
has become a substitute for being and we have
failed on character. We are conformed to the age
but not to the image of God's Son.

Chastisement

Because the Lord loves us He chastens and re-
bukes us. Modern sentimentality has reduced God
to a tolerant indulgent grandfatherly being who
winks at our transgressions.

Children

For this generation, brought up on movie thrillers
and silly comics, I covet a childhood nurtured on
the Word of God. It might seem the depth of boredom to a modern youngster fed on trash and jaded
from worn-out excitements, but life was happier
before the Amen age gave way to the era of So
What.

I am sure that no life is complete that has not known the love of a child. It need not be your own flesh and blood. If you have none of your own, love somebody's child. It is a glorious investment.

Children learn more out of the schoolroom than in it. Indeed, they should bear down on their textbooks, but what they pick up by watching us oldsters and what they glean by the wayside may mean more than what they cram in class.

Choices

God would rather have a man on the wrong side of the fence than on the fence. The worst enemies of apostles are not the opposers but the appeasers.

The greatest choice any man makes is to let God choose for him.

A man never makes a bigger fool of himself than when he settles down in Sodom for personal advantage.

Life is a series of choices between the bad and the good and the best. Everything depends on which we choose. Sometimes the alternatives get in each other's way.

Christ

One of the greatest errors in the church today is the artificial distinction we have created between accepting Christ as Savior and confessing Him as Lord. We have made two experiences of it, but the New Testament makes them one.

We shall find in Christ enough of everything we need for body, mind and spirit to do what He wants us to do as long as He wants us to do it.

You will remember that when Jesus commanded the disciples to launch out into the deep and let down their nets, Peter said, "Master, we have toiled all the night and have taken nothing." Anything that starts with "we" always ends with "nothing" when Christ is not in the boat!

When Christians of Tertullian's day made idols and excused themselves by saying they must make a living he asked, "Must you live?" Some things were more important than life itself and Christ must be Lord of all.

Salvation is not a cafeteria where you take what you want and leave the rest. You cannot take Christ as Savior and refuse Him as Lord and be saved.

We talk much about church loyalty while we beg and coax and almost bribe church members to come to church. People go where they want to go. Where their hearts are their heels will follow. Deeper than church loyalty there must be Christ loyalty and that must grow out of love to Christ.

He is a great Christian in whom Christ is magnified whether by life or by death. I have read of a lamplighter in the old days who went along the street at dusk starting the flame in each of the lamps, fading away in the gathering darkness but leaving the lights he had kindled. So does the true Christian bow out to let Christ take the stage. The friend of the Bridegroom does not steal the show!

Some years ago, two boats were passing each other on the Mississippi, when an old Negro said to a white passenger as he pointed to the other boat, "Look, yonder's the captain!" When asked for an explanation, he said, "Years ago, we were goin' along like this and I fell overboard and the captain rescued me. And since then, I just loves to point him out!"

Often I see the words, "Christ Is The Answer." Indeed, He is the answer to everything. If we are Christians we are members of His body, and therefore part of the answer. But judging by the way some Christians live, they are part of the problem.

"[God] gave him to be the head over all things to the church, which is his body, the fulness of him that filleth all in all" (Eph. 1:22, 23). We are married to Him, members of His Body. Any group that feeds on itself and not on Christ is a monstrosity, for it is a headless body.

My Christ is the virgin-born Son of God who lived a sinless life, died a substitutionary, atoning death, rose bodily from the grave and is coming again to reign.

Christian

God knows His own. It is well that He does, for sometimes it would be difficult for us to determine who are His! Heaven will surprise us both ways.

If you are what you've always been, you are not a Christian. A Christian is a new creation.

The word *Christian* is both a noun and an adjective. We need more *adjective Christians,* more Christian Christians, Christians who are more Christian in thought and spirit and deed as well as in name.

This world is not our home and we lament its sin-wrecked condition, riddled with disease and death and distress. But for the growing of Christian character, it is a proper training ground.

Christians are not citizens of earth trying to get to heaven but citizens of heaven making their way through this world.

I still believe we ought to talk about Jesus. The old country doctor of my boyhood days always began his examination by saying, "Let me see your tongue." That is a good way to check a Christian, the tongue test and what he is talking about.

Too much Christian experience today is second-hand.

After reading impressive church statistics, who can help asking, "With this much salt, why is the country so corrupt? With this much light, why is America in such darkness?" We ought to make a difference.

It is dangerous to grow up next door to Jesus. It is a blessed thing to be reared in a Christian land, in a Christian home, in church and Sunday school, acquainted with the language of the Bible, no stranger to the story of Jesus. But it has its perils. One can live so close to it that the very familiarity breeds an unbelief. Sometimes the most privileged never really know the Savior, whereas others gladly receive Him upon hearing the gospel for the first time.

Christian life is not something we try to live by God's help. Christ lives His life in all who can truly say, "To me to live is Christ."

The Christian life is a matter of coming and going: "Come unto me . . ." (Matt. 11:28); "Go ye into all the world . . ." (Mark 16:15).

Too many Christians live their Christian lives inside their heads; it never gets out through hands and feet and lips.

We sometimes make the Christian life much harder than it is. If it were as difficult to enter into and to walk in as some imagine, most poor souls would give up in despair. I do not understand electricity, but I am not going to sit around in the dark until I do!

The Christian message is Christ come, Christ coming, Christ contemporary. He has come in grace, He is coming in glory, He is with us now.

Using Christian terminology means nothing if one is not a Christian. Having a case of athlete's foot doesn't make you an athlete!

31

The tragedy of modern Christianity is that so many saints are like tourists who stay at home: they read about the Promised Land but they never travel in it. They taste the grapes of Eshcol as some Bible teacher brings them along. They sample the figs and pomegranates in a favorite devotional book. But it is a second-hand experience; they live by proxy a motion-picture life, viewing Canaan from afar, spectators along Jordan's stormy banks.

A husband who is faithful to his wife most of the time is not faithful at all. The term *worldly Christian* is a contradiction. Billy Sunday said, "You might as well talk about a heavenly devil!"

Our Lord would have the Laodicean church be boiling and repentant. Some of us simmer all our lives and never come to a boil.

Christianity

Too much of our Christianity is secondhand. It is like eating canned goods instead of vegetables from your own garden.

A Christian is one who trusts Jesus as his Savior, submits to Him as Lord, and takes the New Testament as the law of his life — all this should happen at the same time. Salvation is not a cafeteria line where you take what you like and leave the rest.

What a host of casual Christian, Sunday-morning saints, to say nothing of the Christmas and Easter variety, who have a superficial interest in "church"! Along with club and lodge and golf and bridge, they manage to include some religion. It is a sideline like stamp collecting or growing African violets. Nothing deep about it, of course. "Oh, dear, we wouldn't think of getting excited about it" — just a cool, mild, casual concern.

In every Christian Christ lives again. Every true believer is a return to first-century Christianity. The problem is how to maintain the simplicity of being just a Christ-ian, an en-Christed one amid the complexity of the modern religious set-up.

America is amusement and entertainment mad, and we have the highest per capita rate of boredom of any people on the face of the earth. There's a delusion going around today, even in evangelical and fundamental circles sometimes, that we must be entertained at church. Christianity has come all the way from an experience to a performance.

We have come to think of revivals as necessary and they are as things now stand, but they were never meant to be. Normal New Testament Christianity is "vival" that does not need constant rekindling. The "malarial"-brand fever followed by chills—is subnormal and abnormal.

The Savior was spoken against (Luke 2:34). His followers were spoken against (Acts 28:22). Christians will be spoken against (Matt. 5:11). The Savior, the sect, the saints—we were never meant to be popular.

Some time ago I watched the great cellist, Pablo Casals, on television; he was teaching a class of advanced students. These young cellists were so good already that they did not seem to me to need any further instruction. But Casals did not feel that way. To one performer he said: "You are playing the notes but not the music!" Something like that is the trouble with modern Christianity. We are playing the notes but not the music, singing the words but not the melody.

To some, Christianity is an argument. To many, it is a performance. To a few, it is an experience.

Christian life

It is high time we learned that in this nerve-wrecking, maddening modern rush, we have let the spirit of the times rob us utterly of meditation, devotion, rest, the passive side of our Christian experience without which we cannot be truly active to the glory of God.

This whole matter of Christian living is simply one issue: believing God.

It is more popular to have special occasions when crowds gather for the spectacular than to major on the day-by-day witnessing of Spirit-filled Christians. There is a place for special efforts. Just because we should be thankful every day does not rule out observing Thanksgiving Day, but too much of our church life today is like doing all our thanksgiving one day in November.

Christians

I have read of a parade of boys in which everyone was in step except one youngster. It was discovered that under his coat he carried a transistor radio, and was marching to other music from a thousand miles away! The Christian is in step with the drumbeats of another world.

We have been saved out of this world; we still must live in the world; we are not of the world; we have been saved to go back into the world to win others out of it, and that is the only business we have in the world!

We are a generation of cheap Christians going to heaven as inexpensively as possible; religious hobos and spiritual deadbeats living on milk instead of meat, crusts of bread instead of manna, as though we were on a cut-rate excursion.

We are at another crossroads. No question is of greater moment than this: shall we let the hostility of this world scare us into becoming diplomats on good terms with the world, the flesh and the devil, instead of flaming witnesses in a head-on collision with a godless age?

God forgive us, in an hour like this, that we have been dry Christians, preaching a dynamite Gospel and living firecracker lives.

My concern is not that most of our people are such worldlings that the cause of Christ does not attract them; it is rather that they are such weak Christians that anything else attracts them!

A "halfway Christian" works both sides of the street. He is religious because it helps him in business and gives him a self-righteous satisfaction. But he has no intention of making Jesus Lord of his life. Yet our Lord said He would rather a man be cold, utterly without profession to be Christian, than medium, lukewarm, "moderate."

Paul was not promised prosperity and popularity in exchange for becoming a Christian. Somehow we have gotten the idea nowadays that when a man becomes a believer or comes to a closer walk with God, that guarantees him promotion and greater success.

We are the salt of the earth, but too much of the salt is content to repose in salt cellars playing church on Sunday morning, when it needs to be shaken out of its smug complacency into the carcass of a putrefying society. We are not meant to be salt depositories but salt dispensers.

God never planned or promised that true Christians would ever be anything more than a persecuted minority, scorning the values of this world and living under rigid discipline, swimming against the stream of this world's thinking and living. As long as they followed that pattern they turned the world upside down.

We are the salt of the earth, mind you, not the sugar, and our ministry is truly to cleanse and not just to change the taste.

God would not have us merely "take a stand," He would have us walk. Too many have taken a stand and are still standing; for years they have made no progress. We are inclined to take a stand and at best strive to maintain it instead of walking daily with God like Enoch.

Christmas

A little girl said she liked Santa Claus better than Jesus because "you have to be good for Santa only at Christmas but for Jesus you have to be good all the time." Much of the Christmas observance at church is not far removed from that attitude.

Christmas is based on an exchange of gifts, the gift of God to man—His unspeakable gift of His Son, and the gift of man to God—when we present our bodies as a living sacrifice.

Church

The Church today numbers one category of Christians whose spiritual experience is wild music without the notes of sound doctrine, a lot of noise that needs a tune. On the other hand, there are thousands who have the notes correct theologically, but there is no melody, no joyous praise, no hallelujah.

The church has no greater need today than to fall in love with Jesus all over again.

We are hearing today about those who like Christ but do not like the church. But Christ loved the church and gave Himself for it. How can we like the Head, but not the Body, the Groom, but not the Bride?

Most people would not want to live where there are no churches but many of them live *as though* there were no churches.

If things are quiet and undisturbed in your church, that is not necessarily a good sign. Things are usually pretty quiet around the sick and the dead and especially in graveyards.

Some churches are merely swapping members, moving corpses from one mausoleum to another. Some have made the Gospel a funeral and others have made it a frolic, and both have forgotten that it is a feast!

Some of our churches are frozen together when they should be melted together. We have plenty of orthodoxy, plenty of teaching, plenty of activity; there is an abundance of good things, and in the midst of it all we are like a cat drowning in cream.

The church is a nursery for babes in Christ but not a hatchery with the idea of taking in bad eggs in the hope that they hatch out into real Christians later. As it is, I could have led many people to Christ — if only they hadn't joined church first.

Any church that has to take a back seat and fearfully anticipate every side show that blows into town is already beaten. We have developed an inferiority complex before the world, the flesh and the devil, and apologetically we take what is left in attendance after our worldly members have gone where they really belong.

Don't ever come to church without coming as though it were the first time, as though it could be the best time and as though it might be the last time.

In other days people chose a church on the basis of their doctrinal convictions. Now, lacking doctrinal convictions, they choose for social reasons.

The meaning of the church is that Christians are God's called-out ones. The mission of the church is to preach the Gospel, to make, baptize, and teach disciples. The message of the church is the Gospel that Christ died for our sins and rose for our justification. The ministry of the church is to observe all things He commanded, and the commandments are summed up in believing on Jesus Christ and loving one another (see 1 John 3:23). Loving others covers all Christian social action.

In the church we have a Christless churchianity and a churchless Christianity, a form of godliness without power, form without force, ritual without righteousness.

One thinks of the dear soul who had changed denominations four times and upon considering a fifth move was reminded by the sagacious old pastor: "Well, it does no harm to change labels on an empty bottle!"

When the pulpit is used to glorify the preacher, when the music only shows off the singers, when church membership only enhances community status, when the prayer house becomes a play house, and when we come more interested in recreation than in re-creation, then the church becomes a house of merchandise.

The church needs time out to tune up. We are so busy building a bigger orchestra that we cannot stop to tune our instruments.

Our greatest hindrance in the church today is within our own ranks. We can't get to the goal for stumbling over our own team. We furnish our greatest interference.

A. J. Gordon once classified some obstreperous church members as "figureheads, soreheads and deadheads." He might have added "Hotheads," of which there is always an abundance.

How we reward and picnic and coax and tantalize church members into doing things they don't want to do but which they would do if they loved God!

43

Most church members live so far below the standard, you'd have to backslide to be in fellowship. We are so subnormal that if we were to become normal, people would think we were abnormal!

Church membership has become a sort of religious credit card that costs nothing in life and will be worth nothing in death.

This much is certain: if we do not soon make church membership mean something, it will soon mean nothing.

There is so little of the miraculous in the church today because most of her members are not living miracle lives.

The church is made of people, and the church is cleansed when we are cleansed. Too many church members, it has been said, have been starched and ironed before they have washed!

If the church of the Acts had overlooked iniquity and by-passed evil and smilingly looked the other way while the devil sneaked into every phase of her life as we have done today, Christianity would have died in infancy.

The church, it has been said, is not running a show-boat but a life-boat, and we make ourselves ridiculous in trying to compete with the world. The preacher and church that stand for God and righteousness will be magnified.

So much "church work" is like a squirrel in a circular cage — plenty of activity but no progress.

When the persecuted become the popular they are powerless. The church prospers in persecution, but pines in prosperity.

It's about time we quit playing church in these services that start at eleven o'clock sharp and end at twelve o'clock dull.

The temple of truth has never suffered so much from wood-peckers on the outside as from termites within.

The church is a soloist, not an accompanist, and was never intended to play second fiddle to political projects disguised as moral issues.

Another thing I liked about Dad at church: he did his sleeping at home. He never used the church for an adult nursery.

The Early Church did something because it believed something. We are trying to do what they did without believing what they believed.

The true church may be driven underground, and if so, may develop more vitality than is now evident above ground. We have come a long way since the church that once suffered in the arena now sits in the grandstand.

The church can stand anything else better than prosperity and popularity. She is poor when she is rich, secure in danger but endangered by security. She usually has most treasure in heaven when she has least on earth.

This is a day of anarchy in the world, apostasy in the professing church, and apathy in the true church.

46

The country church is no mere proving ground for young preachers or dying ground for old ones. There is no more challenging opportunity on any boulevard. Country people are the backbone of the nation.

Salt never did any good in a salt shaker and I have worried about our million-dollar salt cellars on street corners where Christians come to sit but never go out to serve.

Some wayout groups today tell us that they like Jesus but not the church. There are lay movements and extra-curricular organizations today that are not church related. They endeavor to convert people to Christ, but leave them unaffiliated with any local fellowship of Christians. Christ is the Head of the church and the church is His body. We are not preaching the Head without the body or the body without the Head. A bodyless Head is as unscriptural as a headless body. Christ is the Groom and the church is His Bride. We are married to Christ (Rom. 7:4) and espoused to one husband (2 Cor. 11:2). There is no marriage without bride and groom!

47

There are no "inactive" church members. A Negro pastor whose flock numbered one hundred was asked how many active members he had. "One hundred," he replied; "Fifty active for me and fifty active against me."

When comfortable churchmen, secure in their systems, do not welcome the mighty wind of the Spirit because it might disarrange some of their papers and plans and create a new order in which they are not qualified to serve — then it is time for such a fresh breeze from heaven.

Nothing under the sun can be as dry and flat and tedious and exhausting as "church work" without the Spirit.

Citizens of heaven

The Christian moves through the kingdom of this world as a citizen of the Kingdom of God. He is not a citizen of earth trying to get to heaven, but a citizen of heaven making his way through this world.

Civilization

I never say that civilization is going to the dogs. I still have some respect for dogs. Mankind without the grace of God is doing things beneath the dignity of the beasts of the field. I read a story of a hog that got drunk, and when the other hogs would have nothing to do with him, he said, "If you'll excuse me for acting like a man, I'll never do it again!"

Civilizations come and go, and usually they run a cycle from rags to riches to rot.

Psalm 119:126 says, "It is time for thee, LORD, to work: for they have made void thy law." Civilization today reminds me of an ape with a blowtorch playing in a room full of dynamite. It looks like the monkeys are about to operate the zoo, and the inmates are taking over the asylum.

The biggest joke of all is the illusion of progress. One civilization after another has started in hardship, grown rich and rotten and perished — the victim of its own devices.

Classification

We divide humanity horizontally, high class, middle class, low class. God divides vertically, to the right and to the left. He does not recognize neither nor. With Him, we are either or.

Comfort

No journey is complete that does not lead through some dark valleys. We can properly comfort others only with the comfort wherewith we ourselves have been comforted of God.

Comforter

He who becomes a brother to the bruised, a doctor to the despairing, a comforter to the crushed may not actually say much. What he has to offer is often beyond the power of speech to convey. But the weary sense it and it is a balm of Gilead to the soul.

Commandments

We have not learned the commandments until we have learned to do them.

It is a matter of whether one wants to get rich or be rich. We can be rich in Christ Jesus or perhaps get rich in Egypt, but we cannot do both.

You have not really learned a commandment until you have obeyed it. We are His friends if we DO the things commanded. We are to be DOERS of the Word and not hearers only. The church suffers today from Christians who know volumes more than they practice.

Committees

A committee is a group appointed by the unwilling to do the unnecessary!

Communism

Communism sweeps the world because at its center is a hard core of men and women completely sold out to the cause. A real Christian is sold out, not merely to a cause or "church" but to Christ. Is that what you lack?

Companionship

We have the Lord, but He Himself has recognized that we need the touch of a human hand. He Himself came down and lived among us as a man. We cannot see Him now, but blest be the tie that binds human hearts in Christian love.

Compassion

Our Lord worked with people as they were, and He was patient—not tolerant of sin, but compassionate. "A bruised reed shall he not break, and smoking flax shall he not quench" (Matt. 12:20).

Complacency

It is high time that something, persecution if necessary, broke up our complacency and made missionaries out of mere church members.

A complacent fundamentalism needs to get out from under its arbors and trellises, losing its life to find it in evangelizing a lost world!

Complaining

One hour in heaven, and we shall be ashamed that we ever grumbled.

Seen on a church bulletin board: "It takes no musical ability to be always harping on something!"

Compromise

Look out for the compromising spirit. They had that in Pergamos and Thyatira, with the result that Balaam and Jezebel took advantage of a false tolerance and corrupted the life of the church. Sometimes we mistake compromise for charity and put up with what we should put out.

Christianity is not being applied to this age but adapted by compromise with the world, the flesh and the devil.

God despises mixtures. Our Lord says He will spew the lukewarm out of His mouth — and lukewarm is another word for the same state of compromise.

Conversion

Coming to Jesus is a personal matter, not a dry business procedure. Nobody ever fell in love by reading books on how to fall in love.

The tragedy is that so much Christianity today is only a mental acceptance of the gospel — a performance but not an experience.

Diverse are the ways by which men come to Christ. And great is the temptation to judge others if they do not have mud put on their eyes and go to Siloam exactly as we did.

A man can be regenerated, born again, only once, but he can be converted many times. Peter was a believer from the day he followed our Lord in Galilee, but he denied his Lord and for some days he was not a disciple although still a believer. Only after he was converted, turned from his perverse way back into the will of the Master, was he ready to strengthen the brethren and to feed the sheep.

We must improve the present quality of our churches, for converts tend to take on the qualities of the people who convert them.

Conviction

This harassed world seeks refuge in make-believe, in the movies, television, in religious fads, even chemically in drugs. Many people need anything but tranquilizers. They need old-fashioned conviction that keeps them awake all night and makes them miserable until they get right with God.

Country people

If we ever run out of plain country people and reach the day when everybody is a Ph.D., I don't want to be around.

Country preachers and churches

Next to having been a country boy to start with, I am glad that I was a country preacher. I can think of no happier lot for any man. Today your young dominie uses a rural charge as a stepping-stone to town and a retired old preacher may go to such a place to die, so country folks too often put up with ministers too young or too old to be at their mature best. Every preacher ought to serve an internship out among the fields and streams.

Creation

God is not running an antique shop! He is making all things new!

Criminals

The answer to criminality is not recreation, education, or legislation; it is Jesus Christ. If any man be in Christ he is a new creature (see 2 Cor. 5:17).

Criticism

Don't be a quitter because somebody criticizes you. Many a choir singer has performed until somebody hurt her feelings. Then the nightingale became a raven croaking "Nevermore."

Cross

A crossless Christ would mean no more than a Christless cross.

We are not bearing our crosses every time we have a headache; an aspirin tablet will take care of that. What is meant is the trouble we would not have if we were not Christians, the trouble we do have because of our identification with Jesus Christ in His death and Resurrection.

The marks of the cross are simply the marks of our identification with our Lord, death to our own plans and purposes, death to our own right to our lives, that He might have His way with us and ours.

The church has devised a new cross today: an ornament to wear around the neck, a commonplace symbol twisted out of context, a charm, a holy horseshoe. Such an ornament does not interfere with godless living, never goes against the grain of our old nature.

58

We need men of the cross, with the message of the cross, bearing the marks of the cross.

Crucifixion

What an hour! Luther pondered it all alone and at great length while he fasted, and finally arose to say, "God forsaken of God . . . who can understand it!" There are heathen records of an eclipse of the sun at that time. Diogenes witnessed an eclipse and darkness in Egypt and said, "Either the Deity himself suffers at this moment or sympathizes with someone who does." And never forget that while religionists reviled and ridiculed the suffering Savior, a Roman centurion who had never heard a sermon perhaps and had never been in a revival observed, "Truly this was the Son of God."

Cry

People used to weep at funerals and when they got converted; we could stand some of that today in this age that sees something admirable in being dry-eyed stoics ashamed to shed a tear.

Cults

One could spend a lifetime in the study of false cults and isms and never come to the end of it. Rather let him come to know his Bible and his Lord so well, that no false Christ can lead him astray.

Curiosity

Curiosity is not the best motivation for going to church but some come for that reason and see Jesus before they leave. Curiosity put Zaccheus up a tree and Jesus brought him down!

Day-to-day Christianity   Discipleship
Death   Discipline
Deception   Dissension
Decisions   Diversion
Defeated Christians   Doctrine
Deliverance   Doing or dabbling
Demons   Double-minded
Dependability   Doubtful living
Depravity   Dress
Desert   Drinking
Desperation   Dropouts
Devil   Dying
Discernment

Day-to-day Christianity

Occasional high days, answers to prayer now and then, temporary blessings, make an uneven and spasmodic Christian life. But to live day in and out, all kinds of days, in simple dependence on Christ as the branch on the vine, constantly abiding, that is the supreme experience.

Death

I haven't lost Sara [my wife] because I know where she is. You haven't lost anything when you know where it is. Death can hide but not divide.

Jacob buried his beloved Rachel — and journeyed on. When Moses died Joshua took charge and crossed over Jordan. John the Baptist died, and his disciples brought their grief to Jesus. Bring your loss to Jesus, but do not sit up with the past. For He said, "let the dead bury their dead, but go thou . . ."

There is nothing morbid about getting ready to die. For a Christian, it is preparation for life's greatest adventure.

Just as the last day of the year anticipates a new year, so Journey's End for the Christian is but the end of a Prelude. "To depart and be with Christ is far better." There are no "turns for the worse." "To die is gain," so even death is a paying proposition.

And why are so many useful souls taken and use-
less cumberers of the earth left? We know not,
but, after all, that is God's business and we will
not use earth's fleeting time to unravel what only
eternity can reveal.

Deception

We are challenged these days, but not changed;
convicted, but not converted. We hear, but do not
and thereby we deceive ourselves.

Decisions

Joshua made a great speech to the children of
Israel. Near the close of his life he gathered the
people for a farewell message. It has all the marks
of a revival sermon. He began with a rundown of
past blessings. He called upon Israel to renounce
their idols and serve God. It was negative and positive, both barrels of the gun. Then he gave the
invitation to action: "Choose you this day whom
ye will serve" and climaxed it with his own decision, "As for me and my house, we will serve
the LORD." (see Josh. 24:15).

Defeated Christians

Christians are defeated in daily living because they have fought the devil with the weapons of earth: their own resources, will power, moral stamina.

Deliverance

Shadrach, Meshach and Abed-nego had resolved to be true to God and not bow to Nebuchadnez-zar's image. God was able to deliver them from the furnace. "But if not" (Dan. 3:18), they would not bow, come what may. It is well to make allowance that God may not deliver us from the furnace; but He will still deliver us in the furnace. God's people are not promised to be spared suffering. In the world we shall have tribulation and all who will live godly in Christ Jesus shall suffer persecution.

Demons

The only way to meet the modern demon-stration of the powers of darkness is by a demonstration of the power of God.

Dependability

The greatest ability is dependability.

Depravity

I heard of a preacher who had preached a wonderful sermon on, "The Depravity of the Human Heart." Some fellow came down the aisle and said, "I just can't swallow this depravity of the human heart." The old preacher said, "You don't have to swallow it, it's already in you." Brother, we have it whether or not we believe it.

Desert

It is always on the backside of the desert that we come to the mountain of God, on the backside of the desert of self, at the end of our own dreams and ambitions and plans. Moody said that when Moses first undertook to deliver Israel he looked this way and that way (Exod. 2:12) but when he came back from Horeb he looked only one way, God's way. But before he saw God's way he had to come to the backside of the desert.

Desperation

Holy desperation is the door to God's greatest blessings. Those who proved him best in the Scriptures were at the end of everything.

Devil

The devil is the author of a false confidence but he also generates a false diffidence, so that we get vinegar out of what should be wine to our souls.

"Submit yourselves therefore to God. Resist the devil, and he will flee from you" (James 4:7). You have to say "yes" to God first before you can effectively say "no" to the devil.

Some people do not have much trouble with the devil. They are so worthless he doesn't waste time on them.

There is no devil in the first two chapters of the Bible and no devil in the last two chapters. Thank God for a Book that disposes of the devil!

A lot of things seem in the devil's hand but there is no devil in the first two chapters of the Bible and there is no devil in the last two chapters either. He is out of business when the Book closes. Everything is in God's hand, including the future of the devil.

The devil's main business today is getting people to join church without being saved.

Any man who takes Jesus Christ seriously becomes the target of the devil. Most church members do not give Satan enough trouble to arouse his opposition.

Since the quiet hour spent with God is the preacher's power-house, the devil centers his attack on that source of strength.

The old drunkard of years past who became a Christian, changed hitching posts. He no longer hitched his horse at the saloon but at church. Hitching posts have given way to parking meters but still too many church members' cars are found on the devil's territory. Have you changed hitching posts?

The next day after a great day can be a dangerous day. Satan does some of his worst work on exhausted Christians when nerves are frayed and the mind is faint.

Discernment

Nothing is more rare in churches today than discernment. The natural man knows nothing of it, the carnal man is devoid of it. Only the spiritual man has it and we have all too few in that category.

Discipleship

The rich young ruler had morals, manners and money. He would be welcomed readily into many churches today, with no questions asked. He would make a good "joiner," but he would be a poor disciple.

We have put the demands of discipleship in fine print for fear we will scare away "prospects."

The Great Commission bids us make disciples, not merely believers. Jesus was out for disciples, not "joiners."

A believer comes to Christ; a disciple comes after Him. We are long on membership these days, but short on discipleship.

The first item on our agenda is to produce a better grade of Christians before we go out to add more names to our church rolls when we already have too many of the kind we have.

What our Lord said about cross-bearing and obedience is not in fine type. It is in bold print on the face of the contract.

Discipline

Father was the old-fashioned sort who believed that the authority in the home belonged to the parents and not to the children. He was in favor of the posterior application of superior force when necessary.

Dissension

There is so much dissension among the brethren that sometimes one wonders whether he is in the communion of the saints or the confusion of tongues.

Diversion

We can become so upset over world conditions that we forget to preach and live the gospel. We can spend so much time shoveling filth that we bear the smell of it. We can become tainted with what we denounce because some of it always rubs off. If we keep stirring around in garbage and gossip, we end up as trash collectors.

Doctrine

The Bible is simply God's Word about Christ. Christian doctrine is simply systematized truth about Christ.

If the sinner had to wait until he could understand one doctrine of the atonement, let alone get all the scholars together on the subject, he would die in his sins. But the simplest soul can behold one dying on a tree and find life in a look at the Crucified One.

Doing or dabbling

Paul did one thing. Most of us dabble in forty things. Many years ago when I was a dabbling young man, Dr. R. A. Torrey charged me to decide on one thing and stay with it. It was good advice and I have tried to follow it. Are you a doer or a dabbler?

Double-minded

Our yea should be yea and our nay, nay. When I see a dog coming toward me showing his teeth and wagging his tail, I never know which to believe. Let us make up our minds. We are never really neither/nor both. If we are not with our Lord, we are against Him and if we gather not with Him, we scatter abroad.

Doubtful living

Negative, uncertain, doubtful living poisons body, mind, and spirit; fills insane asylums, penitentiaries, graves, hell itself.

Dress

I am always glad to see the end of summer when the populace gets back into its clothes — if not in its right mind.

Drinking

I'm awfully tired of hearing temperance in liquor drinking preached instead of abstinence — as a concession to the cocktail crowd in the congregation.

Dropouts

There are too many "dropouts" in the school of Christ.

Dying

I have read of a poor fellow who was dreadfully seasick. A cheerful soul, such as always shows up at such times, said to the sufferer, "Cheer up, sea-sickness never killed anybody." "Don't tell me that," was the reply. "It's the hope of dying that has kept me alive this long!" The hope of dying can become a welcome prospect to the suffering saint when it means exchanging groans for glory.

The man who is prepared to die is prepared to live.

I heard of a motto that a dyeing business adopted and I thought it was a motto that we Christians should adopt because it relates to the Christian's life so well. The motto read, "We live to dye and dye to live. The more we live the more we dye. The more we dye the more we live."

Easter	Evangelism
Ecology	Evangelize
Economy	Evil
Education	Evolution
Egotist	Excitement
Emotionalism	Excuses
Entertainment	Experience
Eternity	Extremism

Easter

Too many church members wear fancy uniforms, but don't know how to play the game. They look good in a dress parade at Easter, but they smell the battle afar off.

It would be wonderful if Easter crowds thronging the stores for new garments of the season could get as excited about making sure of new garments on that Great Getting-Up Morning!

Ecology

Man has become alarmed over the pollution and the deterioration of our environment and "ecology" has become a familiar word. God spelled it out long ago when He called it "the bondage of corruption" wrought by sin and Satan.

Economy

God hates a false economy that is out to reduce a budget instead of receive a blessing.

Education

Head-knowledge is useful, but unless it is sanctified by the Holy Spirit it can be the most dangerous thing in the world.

Egotist

An egotist is a man who talks about himself so much that you don't have a chance to talk about yourself.

Emotionalism

Too many saints go up like rockets and come down like rocks. They prefer to be flashy comets instead of faithful stars.

Entertainment

A lot of what goes for Bible teaching and evangelism is but religious entertainment. Men are not moved within to the point of obedience.

We are a nation of onlookers, a grandstand generation in the stadium, at the show, at home watching television. The church has become a professional pulpitism financed by lay spectators. Everything is geared to showmanship and entertainment that involves no commitment.

Eternity

Do not so contemplate eternity that you waste today.

Evangelism

Evangelism is the proclamation of the Gospel with the purpose of winning the lost to Christ. Revival is a fresh work of the Holy Spirit among Christians to bring them to confession of sin, renewed dedication and loving zeal for service.

78

Evangelize

The world will not be Christianized but should be evangelized.

Evil

We are not to tolerate evil but abhor it. The mood of the age is to put up with evil, allow it, and then move easily to play with it and finally practice it.

Evolution

The evolutionist thinks we are working our way upward through fetishism, totemism, polytheism, monotheism to the knowledge of God but the Scriptures tell us that we started with a knowledge of God and have been going the other way ever since, not in evolution but in devilution.

79

Excitement

Gipsy Smith, when asked how he kept fresh in soul well into the eighties, replied, "I have never lost the wonder." Thank God for some precious souls who have kept the fire going and growing and glowing.

Excuses

There are no reasons for being a cynic. There are excuses, but an excuse is only the skin of a reason, stuffed with a lie.

The prodigal son could have thought up a list of alibis a yard long in that pigsty, but his salvation began when he resolved to say, "I have sinned." There are many modern prodigals eating husks who have a hundred excuses . . . and they go on feeding hogs. There is no deliverance until we stop passing the buck.

Experience

I remember a motto in an old country doctor's office: "It's what you learn after you know it all that counts!"

This is a day of experts who have all the answers but who don't know what the question is.

Extremism

We go to extremes, we either freeze or fry. Some services are too formal and we come out like ramrods, having mistaken spiritual rigor mortis for dignity. We ought to be dogmatic plus but sometimes we are dogmatic — period. So are there other fellowships coldly orthodox, having the facts but no fire.

We are afraid of extremism, until we are guilty of the worst extremism of all, the extremism of impotence. Some of us are so afraid that we shall "get out on a limb" that we never get up the tree!

Faith	Fighting
Faithful few	Following Christ
Faithfulness	Fools
Familiarity	Freedom in God's will
Family	Friend (unseen)
Favoritism	Fundamentalism
Feasting or nibbling	Fundamentalists
Fellowship	

Faith

We take our faith for granted, and what we take for granted we never take seriously.

I like to make an acrostic of that little word F-A-I-T-H. For All I Take Him. For All I Trust Him. For All I Thank Him. For All He Is I Take Him. For All My Need I Trust Him. For All His Gifts I Thank Him.

Faith will not always get for us what we want, but it will get what God wants us to have.

Faith has no value of its own, it has value only as it connects us with Him. It is a trick of Satan to get us occupied with examining our faith instead of resting in the Faithful One.

Faith has no value save as it links us with God. Yet we often become taken up with our faith and miss God entirely.

It is part of Satan's program to make our faith and practice complicated and involved. Now and then we need a rediscovery of the simplicity that is both in and toward Christ, in Him and in our faith in Him.

Nothing is more disastrous than to study faith, analyze faith, make noble resolves of faith, but never actually make the leap of faith.

I am sure that most of our whining after God to send us some more faith from heaven wrapped and delivered at the door is utterly beside the point. We can WILL to believe and when we do God enables us to exercise faith and even as little as a grain of mustard seed EXERCISED will move a mountain. But we sing about it, talk about it, and never ACT it.

The fable of the mother bear who told her cub, "Shut up and walk!" when he wanted to know which foot to put forward first is a perfect illustration of what we are driving at. Faith in Jesus doesn't wait until it understands; in that case it wouldn't be faith.

What pleases God is faith, and the weakest faith is better than no faith. Faith does not look at itself. Looking unto Jesus we find that He meets our need and proves that we have faith.

A man quietly reading a newspaper may not look as pious as a man on his knees in prayer. But if he has committed his way to the Lord and left it with Him, while he calmly moves on to something else, he is a better Christian than one who never leaves his way with the Lord but is always trying to.

Hudson Taylor worked hard trying to develop faith, until he stopped looking at his faith and learned to rest in the Faithful One. Faith begins by letting go, stretching out on the promises — not by taking a deep breath, clenching your fists, and resolving to trust or bust.

If my faith were so weak that a professor down in Georgia could shake it, I'd get another kind.

Faithful few

Many churches are like an ailing lung with only a few cells doing all the breathing. The real life of the church is in a few faithful people who keep it from being an animated corpse.

A Christian does not have to live — he has only to be faithful to Jesus Christ.

Faithfulness

God called us to play the game, not to keep the score.

Do not let not being able to do it better keep you from doing what you can.

Familiarity

It's a sad day . . . when the Ark becomes a box, and you become so familiar with Scripture and worship and the ordinances that you lose your reverence.

Family

America is a disaster area homewise. The automobile took the family out of the home, and television brought the world into the home.

Favoritism

God has no favorites but He does have intimates.

Feasting or nibbling

Too many Christians are lunching at the cheap counters of this age when they are invited guests to the gospel feast. Others are not worldlings but they are only nibblers, sampling a bit here and there, instead of regular boarders at the King's table. They get a choice morsel from this sermon and another from that book; they even take a square meal once in a while, but their spiritual eating and drinking habits are irregular and spasmodic.

Fellowship

The majority of church members live at such a low standard one would have to backslide to be in fellowship.

Fighting

Some fights are lost even though we win. A bull-dog can whip a skunk but it just isn't worth it!

Following Christ

The Kingdom of God is no place for a man with his face pointed one way and his feet the other. God is not taking people to heaven backwards. One of our biggest problems in the church today is the multitude of church members who have never really made up their minds and set their faces to follow Jesus Christ.

When Cortez and his followers landed in the New World, they burned their ships and so eliminated all means of return to the homeland. Something like this a Christian must do when he sets out to follow his Lord. He must forget the things that are behind. He must let the dead bury their dead. He must put his hand to the plow and not look back. He must set his face like a flint. He must burn his bridges and his boats.

Fools

Some women have made fools out of men. Others have made men out of fools.

We either become fools God's way or stay fools our way.

Freedom in God's will

We can do anything we ought to do, anything He wants us to do. And that leaves plenty of room for miracles! There is wide latitude within the limits of God's will. We shall not feel cramped.

Friend (unseen)

If we are beset by an unseen foe, we are also befriended by an Unseen Friend. Great is our adversary but greater is our Ally.

Fundamentalism

Martha believed in the resurrection as a doctrine, but Jesus would have her see, not a doctrine, but a Person. Much of our fundamentalism needs to move from the doctrinal to the personal and warm its heart in His love.

Fundamentalists

Alas, even fundamentalists are often guilty of sizing and sorting Scripture to fit the dimensions of their own private theories, lopping off this verse and stretching that, to suit the Procrustean bed of some favorite school of interpretation.

We have not gained much by being fundamentalists if we cannot be gentlemen at the same time.

Nobody in pulpit or pew needs a revival more
than a bitter-spirited fundamentalist with his dis-
pensations right and his disposition wrong.

Gift of God	God's provision
Gifts	God's recipe
Givers	God's will
Giving	God's Word
Goals	God's work
God	Good intentions
God's direction	Gospel
God's law	Grace
God's man	Gratitude
God's pilgrim	Great awakenings
God's presence	Greatness

Gift of God

We must stir up the gift of God. Like sugar in the lemonade, it may be there but it needs to be set in motion.

Some stop too soon in their quest for a satisfying experience of the Lord. They get this blessing or that and settle down there and make their blessing an end in itself and a yardstick by which they measure everybody else. The part becomes greater than the whole. They major on the gift instead of on the Giver.

Sometimes your medicine bottle has on it, "Shake well before using." That is what God has to do with some of His people. He has to shake them well before they are ever usable. Paul wrote to Timothy, "Stir up the gift of God, which is in thee."

Gifts

Do not accept gifts that make you beholden to the giver. Satan can close your lips with benevolence from well-meaning but unwise admirers. A free trip to the Holy Land can bind a minister more securely than Delilah tied up Samson.

Givers

We need more people who are more interested in what they can contribute than in what they can collect.

Giving

Much church giving is to ease the conscience. Singing in the choir, teaching a class, giving five dollars, may be only a nice way of "paying off" the Lord while the heart really is set on the concubines of self and sin. It is one thing to write out a handsome check for the church; it is another to give God oneself and the ability by which one earned the check!

Self, service, substance is the Divine order and nothing counts until we give ourselves.

Goals

Some Christians have no goal, some have the wrong goal, some become so occupied with lesser goals that they fail of the main attainment. The means become an end and they stop far short of the best in preoccupation with the good. Churches settle down in new buildings and become Laodicean in lukewarm contentment. Ministers reach a comfortable position and feather their nests so that they no longer fly. The Israelites in Canaan stopped short of victory and did not possess all the land. They ran out of goals. So do we.

It is possible to be defeated by one's secondary successes. Thus the good becomes the enemy of the best and we settle for lesser goals than the heights we might have reached.

God

Isaiah has come to the end of himself. Like Moses and Midian, like Job when he saw God, like Daniel with his comeliness turned to corruption and Habakkuk with rottenness entering his bones; like Peter at Tiberias and Paul with his thorn, he has come to the end of all feeling and trying and praying, the end of all he is and has, to where God begins.

A little boy who had been begging his father for favors all day came once more into his daddy's office. "What do you want this time?" asked the weary parent. "I don't want anything," was the astonishing reply, "I just want to be with you." If our Heavenly Father could be surprised He certainly would be, I am sure, if for once we prayed for no specific needs in particular but only sought His Presence and fellowship.

We are too aware of the "men" in our text and not aware enough of our Father. Our sole business is to glorify Him and so let our light shine that others will glorify Him too.

The only way to hide from God is to hide in God.

I have read of a poor tenement mother whose living quarters were so crowded that she could secure privacy only by throwing her apron over her head as now and then she had a word with heaven. It was a hard expedient, but she had learned that only a step could put her in touch with the eternal.

I get a little weary of these dear souls who have all the dealing and doing of Providence catalogued and correlated and figured out and can give you glib little answers to your heartache. They haven't been far. God just doesn't operate on our time table. And some of His operations don't add up on our computers.

God is our Rewarder but, better than that, He is our Reward.

God does not furnish us with a detailed road map. A traveler in Africa complained to his guide, "There is no road, no path, in this jungle. We have lost our way." The guide replied, "There is no way; I am the way." Our Lord is the Way; when we are with Him, we may not know whither but we know whom.

God works from above with fire from heaven and we put the Gospel to shame by stirring up a fire from our own sparks. Even the world knows the difference, and men only laugh at a church trying to beat the world at its own game. One meeting where God answers by fire is worth all our convocations in the energy of the flesh.

God's direction

If we don't know where we are going, we don't know what to do where we are. . . . Blessed is the man who finds out which way God is moving and then gets going in the same direction.

98

God's law

There is only one explanation for the moral mess we are in worldwide — and it is the worst we have been in since Adam and Eve ate us out of house and home in the Garden of Eden. The cause of the trouble is that we have made void the law of God.

God's man

God is on the lookout for candidates with hearts perfect toward Him. He is not a talent scout looking for somebody strong enough or good enough. He is looking for someone with a heart set on pleasing Him and an eye single to His glory. He will do the rest.

God's pilgrim

God's pilgrim must not only get out, he must go on.

A preacher friend told me that his grandfather used to take him on short trips when he was a little boy. One day when Grandfather asked him to go along, the boy asked, "Where are you going?" Grandfather went on without him and when the boy asked later, "Why did you not take me?" he was told "Because you asked, 'Where are you going?' If you had really wanted to go with me, it wouldn't have mattered where I was going." The pilgrim does not ask God, "Where are you taking me?"

God's presence

We have lost the sense of God in the nation, in the churches, in our lives. The biggest business of the hour is to draw nigh to God that He may draw nigh to us. His presence with us is too often an assumption in our heads instead of an awareness in our hearts.

God's provision

. . . Cherith was the place of God's provision because it was the place of God's purpose. Elijah was in the place where God told him to be. The ravens had been commanded to feed him "there," not somewhere else, not just anywhere, but "there." Where God guides He provides. He is not responsible for expenses not on His schedule. He does not foot the bill when we leave His itinerary.

God's recipe

As a little boy I enjoyed watching my mother make bread or cake. When she assembled the ingredients, they did not look too appetizing. Who wants to eat flour or baking powder? But when she had mixed everything in proper proportions and put them in the oven we awaited the outcome with joy. Sometimes the happenings in our lives are not enjoyable when they come separately one by one. But when God has completed the recipe and put it through the baking, we have "Romans 8:28 cake" and the taste is good, even though some of the ingredients at one time made us weep.

God's will

I am convinced that no man cracks up doing the will of God. He is our Father, not a taskmaster.

I think we sometimes have the impression that God's will is always something we do not like to do. The little boy who said, "This medicine must be good for me, it tastes so bad," was not unlike many Christians in their view of Providence.

Moses did not draw up blueprints of the tabernacle for God to approve. God handed down His plans. Today, we draw up our program and seek Divine endorsement instead of seeking first the Divine program.

God's Word

God's Word is not obsolete, it is absolute.

Hunger for God's Word is not a natural appetite. We are not born with it. It comes with the new birth when we begin with milk and should go on to meat.

God's work

When we get to the place where it can't be done unless God does it, God will do it!

The first thing we need to do in church these days is to discover that God's work must be done by God's people in God's way.

Good intentions

What God looks for is the intent of the heart and, when in our hearts we have already made the sacrifice required, God may sometimes not ask us to actually finish what we meant to do. Abraham put God first, not Isaac, and we read, "In Isaac shall thy seed be called" (Gen. 21:12). Our testimony is perpetuated by the Isaac we offer at God's command, whether consummated actually or intentionally.

Gospel

The fact that the gospel is not popular is all the more reason for preaching it. The very fact that men cannot endure sound doctrine is all the more reason for seeing that they get it. It is not our responsibility to make it acceptable; it is our duty to make it available.

The gospel is for lifeboats, not showboats, and a man must make up his mind which boat he is going to operate.

If it cannot be lived in the shop, there is no sense in preaching it in the sanctuary!

God meant that we adjust to the Gospel — not that we fit the Gospel to us.

When the Gospel hurts the devil's business, trouble begins.

The church is not a glorified glee club staging holy hootenannies and the Gospel was never meant for entertainment.

The Gospel is not a secret to be hoarded but a story to be heralded. Too many Christians are stuffing themselves with Gospel blessings, while millions have never had a taste.

Grace

The grace of God transcends all our feeble efforts to describe it. It cannot be poured into any of our mental receptacles without running over.

We hear these days about "cheap grace." It doesn't mean much to be a Christian. But salvation is the costliest item on earth. It cost our Lord everything to provide it and it costs us everything to possess it.

The man who has been quiet enough to get a message from God will find in the same quiet hour the grace to give it.

Gratitude

We grow up taking things for granted and saving our flowers for the dead. All along the way countless hands minister to our good but rarely do we acknowledge them.

Great awakenings

The great awakenings of the past have been accompanied by preaching *against* sin, and *for* conviction, repentance, godly sorrow, confession and forsaking of sin, restitution, return to first works, return to the Scriptures, and prayer and witnessing and godly living.

Greatness

We are not all made alike and we do not well when we measure by our favorite yardstick. At the last Great Day there will be a big shake-up and a big shake-down. Princes who rode on horses and servants who walked will change places. True greatness in the sight of God will change our little picture of who's who.

Heart	Holy Spirit
Heathen	Homes
Heaven	Human heart
Hell	Humility
Heresy	Husbands and wives
History	Hypocrisy
Holiness	

Heart

It is possible to enjoy preaching as an art without having the preacher's heart. Some of us glory in how much we love church work. Of course, it is well to like what you do, but one may be church-minded without being church-hearted, missionary-minded with being missionary-hearted.

Heathen

There is more hope for an African heathen who has never heard the gospel than for an American pagan who has professed to believe it but has never actually yielded to Christ and been set on fire by the Spirit.

Heaven

A dog is at home in this world because this is the only world a dog will ever live in. We are not at home in this world because we are made for a better one.

Eventually, many of us will meet for the first time, and in Christ we are always sure that Christians never meet for the last time!

We Christians forget so easily that we are not citizens of earth en route to heaven but citizens of heaven temporarily residing on earth.

An old saint was asked, "Would you like to live your life again?" "No," he answered, "I'm too near home!"

Our Savior has gone to prepare a place, but there are places only for those who make reservations. The dying thief made a reservation: "Remember me."

If the fire of hell is not literal, it is worse than actual fire, and if the gates of the Celestial City are not actual gold, they are far finer.

The New Testament writers did not speak of going to heaven so much as going to be with the Lord. It is not the other shore that charms us so much as Jesus on the shore. "Today shalt thou be with me" is what cheered the dying thief more than merely going to be "in Paradise."

Hell

Jesus said that it is better to enter into life crippled than to go to hell whole. Such radical procedure is seldom preached these days and in a very low key if at all. Consequently, we have the frightful tragedy of those who lose everything rather than give up anything, losing all to keep a part.

Heresy

Somehow the idea has gotten around that it is unchristian to take a stand against heresy. Some of us need to read the New Testament again.

History

All we learn from history is that we learn nothing from history.

Holiness

God saved us to make us holy, not happy. Some experiences may not contribute to our happiness, but all can be made to contribute to our holiness.

If you want to be popular, preach happiness. If you want to be unpopular, preach holiness.

For it takes time to be holy, and it takes work, and it takes tears and sweat and travail and study and self-denial and diligent application, and all these things are now out of date.

The old mystics tried to make themselves holier by hiding from society, but living in a hole does not make you holier!

We are weary of the success and happiness school. We need holy men of God who are in touch with Headquarters, who remind us of another world than this.

Holy Spirit

We are not going to move this world by criticism of it nor conformity to it, but by the combustion within it of lives ignited by the Spirit of God.

We say that we depend on the Holy Spirit, but actually we are so wired up with our own devices that if the fire does not fall from heaven, we can turn on a switch and produce false fire of our own. If there is no sound of a rushing mighty wind, we have the furnace all set to blow hot air instead. God save us from a synthetic Pentecost!

111

Some are not filled because they must first be emptied. Even God cannot fill what is already full.

When are we going to learn that all the wonderful things we read about in the Book of Acts were simply the outflow and the overflow of the inflow of the Holy Spirit?

A keen mind and theological training are useful tools when they are sanctified but the Holy Spirit is our teacher and He who inspired the Bible is the best interpreter of it.

There need to be refillings on special occasions. There is a gradual daily growth in grace, but there are special crises that demand special unction.

Homes

The nation is crumbling because our homes have been devalued; what was once a man's castle has become only a place in which to change clothes.

Human heart

One must be up-to-date and current, abreast of what is going on, but the human heart is as always, and nothing really important has changed.

Humility

Jonathan said to David, "I will be next unto thee" (1 Sam. 23:17). The rarest man in the orchestra of God is the saint who knows how to play second fiddle.

He who would call the church back to that brokenness that leads to blessedness must have a broken heart himself. He is not ready to say with Isaiah, "Here am I" (Isa. 6:8) until first he has cried, "Woe is me!" (v. 5). No amount of facts in his head can compensate for lack of fire on his lips.

Husbands and wives

Husbands and wives who would live happily ever after learn early to give and take, to reach agreements by mutual consent. Backbones are indispensable if we are to stand upright, but a man with an unbending backbone is in real trouble. Unmoveable spines lie in graveyards. God made backbones that can bend and also stand rigid.

Hypocrisy

It is an awful hypocrisy that declares with the lips what it denies with the life. The shame of too many church members is that they lead a double life; they fear the Lord and serve their own gods.

Identity

If you try to be everything to everybody, you will end up being nothing to anybody.

Immaturity

One serious malady of the church is infantile paralysis—too many babes who never grow.

Immorality

I used to say that civilization was going to the dogs, but I have quit saying that out of respect for dogs. Today, mankind is guilty of some things beneath the dignity of any dog.

Indecision

It is even better to make some mistakes than to be "a man of two minds undecided in every step he takes." In making a decision, you give God a chance at least to correct it.

Independence from sin

Our Lord offers an Emancipation Proclamation to every slave of sin.

Infirmities

We should glory in our infirmities but not glorify them.

Insomnia

The insomniac cannot sleep, because he tries to hold up the bed. He cannot let go and let the bed hold him up. He may not be lying in a perfect position, but the bed holds him up just the same. Your faith may not be perfect, but God's promises are. You can never trust yourself, but you can always trust Christ.

Investing in the Lord

You really save in this life only that which you spend for the Lord. Under the guidance of the Holy Spirit every expenditure is an investment. The Bank of Heaven is sound and pays eternal dividends.

One feels like stopping some song services where church members sing, "All to Jesus I surrender," "Take my life and let it be consecrated, Lord, to Thee," long enough to ask, "How much can the Lord put you down for? An hour at church, a few dollars in a church envelope?" The test of our affection is how much we will invest in the object of our love.

Invitations

For many years I have given all sorts of invitations but there are some dear souls who never move. There never has been an invitation devised that would touch them. They are like the man in a Kansas revival who told the preacher that he did not want to go to heaven or hell, he simply wanted to live right on in Kansas.

Jesus

Journey

Joy

Judgment

Jesus

A church had a sign in front: JESUS ONLY. One night a storm blew out the first three letters and left US ONLY. Too many churches have come to that.

When Jesus said, "It is finished," the issue was forever settled. God's Son became our sin. We do not settle that issue, but one thing we must settle: what we do about it.

Our Lord is the Bread of Life. His proportions are perfect. There never was too much or too little of anything about Him. Feed on Him for a well-balanced ration. All the vitamins and calories are there.

He must ever have the preeminence for by Him all things consist. The Bible is important but it is only God's Word about Christ. . . . Doctrine is important but a doctrine is just a truth about Christ. Experience is important but an experience is just another step with Christ.

On the night Peter denied Jesus it was a look and not a lecture that sent Peter out to weep bitterly.

It is impossible to do nothing about Jesus Christ. Not to decide for Him is to decide against Him, but decide we must.

Jesus met the devil not in His own name, not in His own power, but with the Scriptures: "It is written. . . . It is written. . . ." If He could defeat the devil with three verses out of Deuteronomy, we ought to be able to do it with the whole Bible.

Jesus is the Divine Physician and Pharmacist and His prescriptions are never out of balance.

A picture of Christ was hung in the back of a pulpit. When the minister rose to speak one Sunday morning, a little boy asked his mother, "Mother, who is that man who stands so we can't see Jesus?"

Some are looking for Jesus — questing for the historic Christ. Some are merely looking at Him as a model, an example. The Christian looks to Jesus for salvation and everything else.

We must get our eyes off our faith and begin "off-looking unto Jesus." We spend much time trying to develop our faith instead of being occupied with Him. Faith grows as we use it for what it is: a means to an end and that end is Himself.

We do not usually learn that Christ is all we need until we reach that place where He is all we have!

Paul's message was always Christ. Never seek satisfaction in any doctrine about Jesus. Press through to Him and touch Him for yourself! And don't spend your time explaining theories about Christ. Present Him. Men are not drawn to a doctrine or a phrase with any lasting profit. The sad finish of many a sect bears ample testimony to that. Don't try to attach people to a phrase; get them joined to Christ through saving faith and they are His to stay!

The popular preacher of my early ministry is unknown today. The in thing then is the out thing now. But we are as dependent on sun and air and water as ever. Jesus preached about simple things and He is still relevant.

Jesus made Himself known only to His own and if others are to hear about Him today you and I must tell them.

We have unwittingly created an artificial distinction between trusting Christ as Savior and obeying Him as Lord. The New Testament recognizes no such false compartments of experience. "Believe on the LORD Jesus Christ," said Paul to the jailer. No man can be a Christian by knowingly and willfully taking Christ on the installment plan, as Savior now, and Lord later.

Let the King take over the little shop of your life and there will be customers! You will be a blessing to others and a workman approved unto Him.

Jesus Christ is the first and last, author and finisher, beginning and end, alpha and omega, and by Him all other things hold together. He must be first or nothing. God *never comes next!*

Journey

The Bible is God's record of man's heartbreaking journey in search of his lost estate. It begins with Paradise lost and ends with Paradise regained.

The hardest part of the journey is neither the start nor the finish but the middle mile. There is the enthusiasm of a new undertaking that buoys you at the beginning and there is the thrill of reaching the goal that carries you down the home stretch; but the middle mile, when you are a long way from the start and home is still distant—that tests the mettle of the traveler.

Joy

Too much church work is being done by people who are not right with God and each other, who know neither the joy of salvation or a willing spirit.

There is much artificial whipped-up joy among Christians today, the same sort of enthusiasm that can be worked up at a ball game by a cheerleader. There is not enough of our Savior's joy, which should remain in us and be full—the kind that Paul had when he wrote, "Rejoice in the Lord always: and again I say, Rejoice."

Because of our shallow living we know little of Christ, so we work hard trying to pump up a substitute. How much of our religious life today runs on the same stimulus that a sporting event produces! But it is a poor substitute, it has a hollow ring and it gives out when we need help most.

Judgment

There is a comfortable attitude about Jesus Christ in our churches today, and it is our greatest peril. After all, we are not judged so much by how many sins we have committed but by how much light we have rejected.

In this day, when law and order seem on the way out and criminals get only a slap on the wrist, it is well to remember that the wages of sin remain the same and what men sow they still reap.

Kingdom work
Knowledge

Kingdom work

If we stopped half of our feverish and futile "kingdom work" without the King and repaired God's altars and sought the old-time power, we would need no argument to convince an unbelieving world that "the Lord, he is the God."

Knowledge

Some things are for us to know, some things are not for us to know. Blessed is the man who learns early which is which. Most of our unhappiness is caused by not knowing what we should know and by trying to know what we are not to know.

God does not tell us all we want to know about anything, but he will tell us all we need to know.

We know too much. We have read and heard everything. The happiest person is a young Christian before he has met too many Bible scholars! We need more than anything else some plain and simple Christians who will let God be true and every man a liar.

We know enough to set the world on fire but while our heads are filled with loads of learned lumber our hands have never built anything with it. The need of the hour is a first-class, heart-felt experience of the Lord that gets into our hands and feet.

Last days	Listening
Law	Living
Learning	Living sacrifices
Leisure	Lord's Day
Liberalism	Lordship of Christ
Life	Lost
Lifestyle	Love
Light	Loyalty

Last days

Has there ever been a day when more people talk and come and sit at church and hear, only to do nothing about it? This, of course, fits into the scriptural picture of the last days with a form of godliness denying the power thereof.

Law

There's no regard for the law of God. I heard of a family on a picnic some time ago. When the boy stole a watermelon out of a patch nearby, his mother said, "Don't you get another one. You don't know what they've been sprayed with."

We do not really break the laws of God, we break ourselves against them. We do not break the law of gravitation by jumping from a skyscraper, we break our necks. Franklin said, "He who spits against the wind spits in his own face." Our sins find us out.

Learning

The crying need with most of us is not so much to learn more as to unlearn much of what we already know.

130

Leisure

Learn a lesson from leisure. "Everlastingly at it" will bring you only high blood pressure and apoplexy. Learn to read both ways as you go through the book of life. What you cannot find by digging you may discover by browsing.

Liberalism

Liberalism is not the answer to a heart longing for a vital faith.

Life

We've learned how to lengthen life, but we don't know how to deepen it. You would have to live twice as long to live half as much as your fathers.

Life is like a grain of wheat: to plant it is to recognize its value; to keep it is to destroy its value. The "planted" Christian counts life dear not unto himself but unto God.

An irate woman met her husband when he got off a merry-go-round and said, "Now, look at you: you spent your money, you got off right where you got on, and you ain't been nowhere!" It is a perfect picture of modern living.

Survival is no longer the main issue with us senior citizens. Our life span has been lengthened, and machines keep us overtime. What matters most is the quality of life.

A ninety-year-old man was leaving on a trip around the world. An old friend lamented, "You ought not to try a trip like this. I might not see you again." The departing gentleman replied, "Maybe not. You may be dead when I get back!"

Lifestyle

There is not much connection between what most of us do at church on Sunday, and the way we live the rest of the week.

Our heads are traveling by fast express these days, and our hearts follow by slow freight.

A man came home from the office one evening lamenting: "We had a rough day, the computer broke down and everybody had to think."

Light

Do you remember walking across a field on a sunny day and turning over a large stone? What happened? Why, the moment the light struck the ground beneath it, all the creeping and crawling things began hurrying and scurrying for cover. This is just exactly what happens to our sinful hearts. There is an uneasiness when we face up to the light of Christ.

We are not here to learn how to live in the dark but to walk in the light. We are not here to get along with evil but to overcome it with good.

Listening

Two little girls were looking at the great picture of Christ at the Door. One asked the other, "Why don't they let Him in?" The other replied, "Maybe they're down in the basement and can't hear Him!" Too often we are down in the basement of our lower selves, the cellars of sin, and we hear not His voice. The big question today is not, "Is God speaking?" but "Are you listening?"

Living

A Christian ought to live with a sense of wonder, always expecting God to do some marvelous thing. We really do not expect much from God these days. We pray for rain and leave our umbrellas at home. We pray for revival but don't really expect one to start today. We have been told that whatsoever we ask in prayer, believing, we shall receive, but we ask, doubting, or, at the most, we ask, merely hoping, and our expectation is not unto Him.

One can make a closer walk with God tomorrow his goal so ardently that he does not walk with Him today.

There is the sad mistake of feeding on devotional books and chasing one Bible teacher after another without living daily as much of that life as we already know. There is such a thing as setting out grimly to live a maximum Christian life instead of enjoying daily the grace that is ours now. We never learn it all so let us make much of our present experience.

Living sacrifices

(God) wants our bodies as living sacrifices, not corpses.

Lord's Day

It is not the day that is so important but the God who made it.

135

Lordship of Christ

Jesus Christ demands more complete allegiance than any dictator who ever lived. The difference is, He has a right to it.

The heart of revival, of the deeper Christian life, of Christianity, is making Jesus Lord.

If I had only one sermon to preach it would be on the Lordship of Christ. When we get right on that point we are right all down the line. God honors the exaltation of his Son.

Has He taken over in your heart? Perhaps He resides there, but does He preside?

Lost

The word "lost" has almost disappeared from our vocabulary and any mention of eternal punishment is smiled away as a leftover from a dark theological past.

I remember when the Titanic sank in 1912, it was the ship that was supposed to be unsinkable. The only thing it ever did was sink. When it took off from England, all kinds of passengers were aboard—millionaires, celebrities, people of moderate means, and poor folks down in the steerage. But a few hours later when they put the list in the Cunard office in New York, it carried only two categories—lost and saved. Grim tragedy had leveled all distinctions.

Love

We have left our love for Christ, and when love for Christ dies, love for each other, for the Bible, for souls, dies.

Our Lord spent a lot of time eating and visiting with common folk to teach us that love is proven more by etiquette than by eloquence.

What we love usually manages to get into our conversation. What is down in the well of the heart will come up in the bucket of the speech.

Loyalty

A wife who is 85 percent faithful to her husband is not faithful at all. There is no such thing as part-time loyalty to Jesus Christ. It is all or nothing.

Man	Missions
Marching to the gospel	Mistakes
Marriage	Moderatism
Materialism	Modernism
Medals or scars	Modern living
Meditation	Monotony
Members	Morals
Memories	Moses
Message	Mother
Ministers	Motive
Ministry	Music
Minors	Mystery
Miracles	Mystics
Missionaries	Myths

Man

History is the long story of man trying to be God. He has been at it ever since Satan brought about his fall in Eden.

God is on the lookout today for a man who will be quiet enough to get a message from Him, brave enough to preach it, and honest enough to live it.

Marching to the gospel

Don't be afraid to be out of step. This world has to square with the gospel.

Marriage

Some poor mortals may have been married under orange blossoms and found they had a lemon just the same, but they should not bore the rest of us because of their misfortune.

140

Switch two letters in the word "united," and it reads "untied."

Marriage has been reduced to a joke and is no longer a lifetime contract. We have cheap marriages and cheap homes because there are too many cheap people who lack the integrity to keep any contract.

The cause of broken marriages is selfishness in one form or another.

Materialism

Patrick Henry asked, "Give me liberty or give me death," but modern Americans simply say, "Gimme."

Medals or scars

Where are the marks of the cross in your life? Are there any points of identification with your Lord? Alas, too many Christians wear medals but carry no scars!

Meditation

It is next to impossible to find a quiet place for meditation these days. If you do not carry a calm spot in your soul, it will not help much to find one on the outside.

I would say to today's young minister, "Be not afraid to give much time to solitary walks and meditation."

Members

Church members too often expect service and never think of giving it.

Memories

Memory can become a tyrant instead of a treasure chest. From the mistakes of the past, let us learn whatever lessons they teach, then forget them, even as God remembers our sins no more. Let precious memories be benedictions but not bonds.

142

Message

You and I are human post offices. We are daily giving out messages of some sort to the world. They do not come from us, but through us; we do not create, we convey. And they come either from hell or from heaven.

Ministers

A minister should go to every service as though it were the first, as though it could be the best, and as though it might be the last.

A minister may have his study walls lined with diplomas, his ordination papers signed by illustrious men, a sheaf of recommendations from the mighty of the land, but if the stamp of heaven on his commission is faint and fading, he had better close up shop and take time out until he can return to his pulpit with a brand-new autograph from God. When he is thus re-signed, he will be reassigned, like Elijah, like Jonah, like Peter. He may be given the same task, for some churches need not a new preacher, but the same preacher renewed.

I would venture a word to young Timothys: Do not make cronies of any of your flock for your buddy may turn out to be your biggest problem. Do not talk your views, preach them. Dr. Jowett expressed himself from the pulpit but had little to say in general conversation.

Some old ministers think it is their duty to sit in a corner and let youth have its day. They offer no counsel, utter no warning, and remain silent on burning issues; they consider that a mark of Christian graciousness, but they miss the opportunity to render a great service.

Ministry

This is our real "Program": faith in Christ, fellowship with Christ, faithfulness to Christ, fruitfulness for Christ.

Minors

I have heard also of "wearing a sailor suit to cross a creek." We give too much importance to lesser matters, make a big show out of small performances, burn up a gallon of energy on a pint-size project. We dress up mint, anise and cumin and neglect judgment, mercy and faith. It is like working up a mass parade and staging fireworks just to campaign for dogcatcher.

Miracles

You may be beating grain on a threshing floor, grieved over the times and wondering where God and His miracles are, but that is better than not expecting miracles at all.

Too many times we miss so much because we live on the low level of the natural, the ordinary, the explainable. We leave no room for God to do the exceeding abundant thing above all that we can ask or think.

Most of us Christians are living way below the miracle level. We can explain everything that happens by ordinary cause and effect.

Some say that to believe the Bible miracles would mean intellectual suicide for them. If all who complain that way did commit such suicide, it would not be a major disaster!

The average run-of-the-mill Christian today believes that God can do miracles, but few think He will in any given case.

Peter had no money to offer but he performed a miracle. The church today no longer says, "Silver and gold have I none," but neither can she say, "Rise and walk." Men, money, movements, there are aplenty but few miracles.

When Jesus performed a miracle, He sometimes said, "Don't tell it." He performed miracles but didn't advertise them; we advertise them and don't perform them.

146

Missionaries

We are like a roomful of lamps all brilliantly lighted and trying to outdazzle each other on Sunday. We enjoy our own company so much that we become members of an exclusive club, instead of missionaries.

Some missionaries bound for Africa were laughed at by the boat captain. "You'll only die over there," he said. But a missionary replied, "Captain, we died before we started."

Missions

We can go to the mission field in person, by prayer, by provision, or by proxy as we help send someone else. But there is a mission field across the street as well as across the sea. And perhaps the most urgent mission field right now is the membership of the average church.

Mistakes

Blunders we shall make and failures will shame our faces and dampen our eyes. But if we can manage not to remember what we ought to forget and not to forget what we ought to remember, then forgetting the things behind and stirring up our minds by way of remembrance, we shall press on for the prize.

Moderatism

Moderatism slaps God on the back in cheap familiarity; it makes Christianity a cheap commodity. Moderatism is the product of this age of conformity, peaceful co-existence.

Modernism

What we need is not something new but something so old that it would be new if anybody tried it! A return to the principles, program, and power of the old faith would be the greatest of innovations! Church services would not resemble the average meetings today. Nothing would be newer than the old faith if we gave it a chance.

Modern living

We have never lived so close together — and so far apart.

Monotony

Monotony wears down the spirit and may be harder to master than times of crisis. We can be bored to death! It just takes longer! But faith can serve God without feeling until better days return.

Morals

It would take a moral and spiritual earthquake to undo the mistakes of the past fifty years in home discipline, in education, and in religion. One wonders whether we have reached the point of no return.

Moses

"Moses wist not that . . . his face shone," (Exod. 34:29). The hypocrites were conscious of a sad face; Moses was unconscious of a shining face. Think it over.

Mother

Mama was one of the best Christians I ever knew. She was timid and shy and let Dad do most of the talking at home and abroad. She could sit in the old-time revivals in the little country church when we had a shouting time and everybody got happy but she didn't join in. She believed in it and enjoyed it but it just wasn't her way.

Motive

Sometimes we drive the automobile into the repair shop and say, "Check the motor." It is time we church workers drove into God's repair shop and asked Him to "check the motive." Why do you do what you do in church?

We live in a world order as rotten as Sodom ever was. Civilization is doomed to judgment. . . . We are not here to save civilization. God is calling out a people for His Name.

Music

The distemper has invaded the churches in what goes for gospel music. It would be bad enough if jazz had remained in the night clubs amidst the darkness of heathenism. . . . But when the church borrows both the language and the livery of Sodom, it is time to hang our heads in shame.

One frequently meets passersby with music emanating from transistor radios on their persons. Lacking music in our hearts, we carry it in our pockets!

Mystery

A mystery in the New Testament is not a glorified puzzle but rather something which we never would have known had not the Holy Spirit revealed it.

Mystics

Some of the old mystics were really mistakes. They tried to be more saintly by hiding in caves. Living in a hole never made anybody holier.

Myths

If the creation story, the virgin birth, the resurrection are only myths, then I'm myth-taken and myth-ified, and mytherable!

Nature

New Christians

New Year

Nature

God made the country and man made the town —
and you certainly can see the difference!

New Christians

Let us remember how we loved Christ as young Christians when we were the happiest people in the world, before we met too many Bible scholars and saw too many church members! Remember our sweetheart love for the Lord before it degenerated into cold orthodoxy and mechanical church work.

Christians are not just nice people. They're new creatures. If you are what you have always been you are not a Christian. A Christian is something new; old things have passed away and all things are become new.

New Year

For the Christian, there is not only a New Year on the calendar but a New Forever in the heart!

While the world drinks and dances into the New Year to spend tomorrow with a hangover, let the Christian meet it on his knees and meet tomorrow with a hallelujah!

Obedience

Optimism

Ordinary people

Organization

Outdoors

Obedience

When God bids you dip in Jordan, wash in Siloam, or walk a desert trail, the victory lies at the end of that venture. When God says, "Go!" that is not a suggestion but a command.

We are always making an offering. If we do not give to God, we give to the devil. It is a continuous process going on all the time.

Optimism

We need to get our eyes cleared up. You can't be optimistic with a misty optic. Get your eyes open, and when you do, you'll see that "there are more with us than they that be with them," as Elisha told his servant.

Ordinary people

Revivals make headlines, but when the books are added up at the last day, it will be found that the main work was done by the faithful preaching of ordinary pastors, the daily witnessing of ordinary Christians, and soul-winning in home and church.

Organization

It is the day of the organization man and we are as alike as eggs in a crate — rubber stamped, numbered, tagged and labeled from A to Z, from Automobile license to Zip Code. It will end in the last big number, 666, the mark of the Beast.

Outdoors

The outdoors played a big part in the life of Bible prophets. Even Paul, who was a city man, prepared his theology in the deserts of Arabia. I am convinced that many of our distempers would vanish if we could escape outdoors. I am sure that the devil has no more effective device for crippling preachers than to tie them up as Delilah did Samson with a thousand little duties until they are reduced as Samson was to a treadmill, and the Spirit of the Lord had departed.

Paperbacks	Preachers
Paradise	Preaching
Parenting	Present
Pastors	Pressure
Peace	Pride
Pentecost	Priorities
Perfection	Prodigal son
Perplexed	Progress
Persecution	Promises
Pilgrims	Prophets
Playing it safe	Prosperous
Praise	Provoke
Prayer	Purpose

Paperbacks

I was riding along a highway the other day and saw a sign, "Dirt for sale." I said, "They ought to hang that over every rack of paper-bound books in the drugstores of America." Not since Manhattan Island was sold for $24 has there been so much dirt available for so little money as now.

Paradise

There has been much speculation about Paradise, what and where it is. I shall know that in due time but meanwhile what matters most is that He said, "Today shalt thou be WITH ME." I am not so concerned with WHAT is there as I am interested in WHO is there. "Where I AM, ye may be also" . . . it is Who He is that makes heaven what it is.

Parenting

My father could talk it, and, by the grace of God, he lived it. He had not only a talking but a "walking" knowledge of the Scriptures.

My father considered himself to be the head of the family, and the rest of us were inclined to agree with him. He was not opposed to the posterior application of superior force, if necessary. He was not afraid he would frustrate Junior. He saw no conflict between love and discipline. Neither does the Bible. Our Lord said, "As many as I love, I rebuke and chasten" (Rev. 3:19).

Pastors

A true pastor must not only feed the flock, he must warn the flock. He must not only be zealous but jealous (2 Cor. 11:2).

Many a church thinks it needs a new pastor when it needs the same pastor renewed.

Do not dwell in your ivory tower and neglect the flock, but do not become so involved with your flock that you cannot be a prophet on Sunday. I have seen good men become the flunkeys and bellhops of their congregation.

Peace

God's answer tells why. We will not have peace without righteousness. We will never get rested until we get right.

Jeremiah writes of false prophets "saying, peace, peace, when there is no peace." It is a mark of the times that the less peace there is, the more we talk about it.

Men do not have peace in the world nor in their hearts because they do not have peace with God. Nothing is settled until it is settled right and nothing is settled right until it is settled with God.

"There is no peace . . . to the wicked." The world offers false peace to dull the senses, deaden the conscience, quiet the nerves, but it cannot give peace.

Pentecost

Long ago Lorenzo of Florence put on a pageant of Pentecost. He had the twelve apostles lined up down front and at a given time real fire was to fall. But something went wrong. The fire fell but the apostles were set aflame, the curtains ignited, the building caught on fire and the people barely escaped with their lives. Something like that always happens when we try to stage a synthetic Pentecost!

Perfection

Too many churches have begun in the Spirit and are trying to perfect themselves in the flesh.

Perplexed

Because some things do not make sense to us now does not mean that they never will make sense.

163

Because things do not make sense to us does not mean that they don't make sense at all.

Jacob said, "All these things are against me." But Jacob was mistaken, for all things cannot be against us if all things work together for good.

Things which don't make sense to our ordinary reasoning can make sense to our spiritual understanding even now.

Persecution

The gospel thrives on persecution. It makes better headway against a world that fights it than against a world that trifles with it. Bitter hostility is better than half-hearted endorsement.

The modern church member all too often avoids persecution by taking the line of least resistance and living in a truce with this age. The early Christians wore scars but we wear medals.

Pilgrims

This world is not our rest. We have here no continuing city. This is the house of our pilgrimage.

Playing it safe

The rich young ruler had much but was aware of a lack. Lacking one thing, he really lacked everything. He needed to "sell out" for Jesus Christ. He was "playing it safe" but never is a man so unsafe. A lot of nice people with fine moral records are in his plight.

Praise

You cannot change the order of penitence, person, praise. When God's people repent and give themselves to God they will have a song. It will be spontaneous, for what is down in the well will come up in the bucket.

Prayer

If you can't pray like you want to, pray as you can. God knows what you mean. And you have good help—the Advocate who is God's Son and the Paraclete who is God's Spirit. They will take your feeblest prayer and make it perfect.

The devil is in constant conspiracy against a preacher who really prays, for it has been said that what a minister is in his prayer closet is what he is, no more, no less.

Prayer may not get us what we want, but it will teach us to want what we need.

The Holy Spirit prays for us with unutterable groanings. If He groans for us, we might well agonize in prayer for ourselves!

The measure of any Christian is his prayer life.

We may get a secret satisfaction out of praying that makes prayer only an end in itself. "Early will I seek Thee"—that is true prayer.

God is not impressed by length or loudness in our prayer. He sees the heart and when we have prayed our hearts into acceptance of His will and our wills into obedience to it, we may calmly wait for the answer.

The thermometer of a church is its prayer meeting.

Many a man who would never think of dashing out in the morning without his breakfast, his vitamins and his briefcase, plunges headlong into a perilous day with an unprepared soul. "A little talk with Jesus" readies the body, the mind and the spirit for whatever comes.

Rummaging through my father's papers the other day, I came across this old well-worn statement: "Nothing is ever settled till it is settled right, and nothing is ever settled right till it is settled with God." God invites us to talk it over: "Come now, and let us reason together" (Isa. 1:18).

Preachers

If a preacher is not doctrinally ready to preach, he is not ready.

If we preach the whole counsel of God, we shall be accused of extremism, not only by the world but also by a professing church that cannot endure sound doctrine.

A preacher should have the mind of a scholar, the heart of a child, and the hide of a rhinoceros. His problem is how to toughen his hide without hardening his heart.

The preacher who will not preach his heart out before a few people would be no good before a multitude.

It is not enough to love to preach. We must love those to whom we preach, and such love is a practical thing.

There's a new variety of preacher today who's not interested in being called "a holy man of God." He wants to be called by his first name and be just one of the boys. He's so anxious to be relevant that he's forgotten how to be reverent. I never cared for "Reverend" as a title, but it does indicate some respect.

168

A preacher who is too big for a little crowd would be too little for a big crowd.

If you would try out a preacher, send him to preach to farmers: if he cannot make the grade there, let him reconsider his call—or maybe he needs to be converted.

We need to recall our first love, when we were converted, called to preach, when we were in our first pastorate, before we had seen so much evil and had been disappointed in men we once respected and had the Spirit quenched in us until our consecration threatened to become cynicism.

When a famous preacher arises, swaying the crowds, one by-product is that some of his contemporaries begin to imagine that they must be out of God's will or not filled with the Spirit because they are not achieving similar results.

A country schoolteacher, applying for a job, was asked, "Do you teach that the earth is round or flat?" "Which way do you want it taught?" was the reply. "I can teach it either way." Something like that is the attitude in many a pulpit today.

169

What breaks preachers down is not doing God's will, but rather, doing what we want to do, or what people think we should do. God is our Father, not our taskmaster, and He never lays more upon us than we can do by His Spirit.

We ministers sometimes forget that our Lord runs the preaching business. We are tempted to pull wires and do a little politicking and we try to slap backs and know the right people, and make contacts in order to promote our ministry. If we spent less time recommending ourselves to the brethren and more time showing ourselves approved unto God, the Lord of the Open Door would open doors no man can shut.

The task of the preacher is to comfort the afflicted and afflict the comfortable.

Anything can happen in the life of a preacher and it usually does! It has been said that a preacher must be ready to die, ready to preach, and ready to take up a collection. He must be ready for any eventuality, geared to surprises, set for emergencies. He must control his emotions to meet tragedy or comedy.

No man can preach if he confers with flesh and blood for his authority.

Unwittingly, the church conspires to rob the preacher of his power, demanding of him such a multitude of small performances that on Sunday he cannot preach at all. To relieve that dilemma, the booksellers supply him with a manual for the year with sermons for both morning and night. Grasping at that, he who began as a preacher ends as a phonograph, reciting mail-order sermons that never breathed the breath of life.

Preaching

I trust I am not one who pounds because he can't expound.

Make Jesus Christ your theme! I have seen preachers espouse causes and champion movements, and when the cause died and the movement collapsed, the preacher vanished too. But the man who glories in Christ never grows stale.

One should enter the pulpit as though it were the first time, as though it could be the best time, and as though it might be the last!

Preaching the truth makes people either sad, mad, or glad. Too many people today leave church on Sunday neither sad, mad, nor glad; they go out as they came in. Better go out mad than just go out!

I've never done any politicking to get to preach anywhere. You don't need to know key men to get along. You need to know the "Keeper of the Keys."

We have suffered from the preaching of cheap grace. Grace is free, but it is not cheap. People will take anything that is free, but they are not interested in discipleship. They will take Christ as Savior but not as Lord.

People do not like to be called to holiness and righteousness and will not flock to the prophet who calls to a straight and narrow way. It costs to do that kind of preaching.

An awful lot of preaching misses the mark because it proceeds from love of preaching, not love of people.

I preach on specific sins because people are not convicted by sermons on sin in general. It was when our Lord said to the Samaritan woman, "Go call thy husband . . ." (John 4:16), that she really faced up to her sinfulness.

Pity the preacher who uses a text only as a launching platform from which to blast off into space, departing therefrom and never returning thereto! There is a power in the direct preaching of the Bible that attends no other pulpit exercise.

I never knew the day when I did not feel that I should preach and write. I memorized Bible portions, made little Sunday school talks, and sent my first "sermon" to our small-town newspaper when I was nine.

God pity the preacher who has grown cross-eyed watching certain faces in his congregation to observe whether the message is acceptable or not. "The fear of man bringeth a snare" (Prov. 29:25), and the chilly countenances of resentful listeners who must not be disturbed have taken the heart out of more preachers than have all the infidels and higher critics.

A preacher once put his hand down on a wasp in the pulpit and let out a yell that could be heard all over the churchyard. One listener in the congregation nudged his companion and said, "I'm going to like this preacher!"

While we do lament sometimes how far short the best have fallen, we ought to rejoice in the bad that has become good, and in the good that has become better.

I have sought to emphasize certain themes — revival, discipleship, the Lordship of Christ, the filling of the Spirit, the Lord's return. I have endeavored to call preachers to more meditation and reflection and solitude in this harassed and ear-splitting day.

Some preach the truth and don't have love. Some preach love and don't have the truth. Get the mixture right. The truth will keep you from dissolving into sentimentality; love will keep you from hardening into severity.

174

Present

How many of us live looking back or ahead, between a holy past and a holier future, but in a hollow present!

Pressure

The victorious life is not attained in some peaceful retreat away from the noise and the sin. It is not secured by religious tranquilizers or by singing, "Relax, my soul, calm every nerve." Our Lord was under constant pressure throughout His ministry. His peace is ours in the midst of the conflict and we can be at rest within while we work without. We need to go apart and rest awhile whenever we can, but not so much to escape the pressure as to refresh our spirits before we return to it. We can have peace under pressure and triumph amidst the tribulation.

Pride

God selects some of all strata whether fishermen or fanatics, but not many wise, mighty, and noble so that no flesh should glory in His presence.

Every Christian is a priest, not offering a sacrifice for sins — since that has been done once and for all — but offering his person, praise, and possessions.

I recall the sinking of the Titanic in 1912, that early object lesson of the unsinkable ship that sank on its maiden voyage. What a rebuke to our pride, but we learned nothing from it!

Priorities

Many a man called to be a preacher wears out in trivial missions, not necessarily evil, but not worth his time and effort. It is important to get our priorities in place.

Prodigal son

The far country is not hard to find. You can enter it right where you are; you do not have to go to Las Vegas. It is a state of the mind, of the heart and of the affections. It is rebellion against the Word and will of God.

Progress

Progress is a farce because man's head and hand have created wonders that stun the imagination, but his heart does not keep step and his morals undo all that his mind has wrought.

Progress as we know it is a myth. Man is not evolving upward toward a knowledge of God. He started with a knowledge of God and has been going the other way ever since.

No one has time anymore for all the leisure that automation is supposed to give us. When have you seen anybody just walking and thinking? Along a highway these days such a curiosity would be judged either out of his head or out of gas.

Promises

There are sickly Christians living on crackers and cheese when they have a standing invitation to the feast of the grace of God.

His promises are checks to be cashed, not mere mottoes to hang on the wall!

Prophets

The prophet is a troubleshooter, not a trouble-maker.

It is a mark of the prophet to make men face sin.

There is great need today for the New Testament prophet who speaks to edification, exhortation, and comfort, a strengthening, stirring and soothing ministry.

God calls prophets to awaken all resters-at-ease in Zion. They are not troublemakers but trouble-shooters who have a genius for locating bugs in the machinery and a gift for exposing them.

Prophetic truth calls us not only to preparation and expectation but also to purification: "And every man that hath this hope in him purifieth himself, even as he is pure" (1 John 3:3).

178

Great emphasis is being given to the pastor as the "equipper" of the laymen for their ministry (Eph. 4:11, 12). This is part of his work, but he also has a prophetic ministry which is fast disappearing as prophets become priests.

Prophets are almost extinct in the religious world today. The modern church is a "non-prophet" organization.

I would say to preachers: beware of the disarming effect of too much familiarity with and too many favors from your congregation. Many a prophet is silenced by the kindnesses of his people. Popularity has killed more prophets than persecution.

The prophet is essentially a rebel. Rebellion may be either bad or good. Satan was a rebel against God and was cast out of heaven for it. But rebellion can be good. Jesus was a rebel against the lifeless established religion of His day. So were Paul and Luther and Knox and Wesley and all who clash with the established order of their time.

Prosperous

God wants no man to be any more prosperous than his soul.

Provoke

We provoke one another but not to love and good works!

Purpose

Moving all the while and getting nowhere is not confined to rockers; plenty of people live that way.

Quiet hour

Quiet hour

There is no work more likely to crowd out the quiet hour than the very work that draws its strength from the quiet hour.

We Christians have allowed this crazy age to steal from us the quiet hour. We too have been caught in the whirl, and we cannot minister to others because we are as tired and feverish and hurried as the world.

Redemption	Rest
Regeneration	Results
	Resurrection
Religious business	Revelation
Religious rut	Reverence
Renewal	Revival
Repentance	Riches
Reputation	Risk

Redemption

Salvation is free but not cheap. The gift of God cost God His Son, His life. With His own precious blood He bought us in the market, bought us out of the market, bought us never to return to the market. We are not redeemed by anything we are or have or can do.

The fare was paid at Calvary and modern self-sufficients want to pay their own way. They do — but they arrive at the wrong destination.

Regeneration

There are too many religious Sauls who need to become regenerated Pauls asking, "Lord, what wilt thou have me to do?"

Religious business

We spend much time today trying to arouse indifferent church members to do religious work, time that could be spent more profitably in getting them right with God and each other. After that, they are ready to go to work. Simply recruiting more Ephesians to more works and more labor without their first love only worsens a situation that is bad enough now.

184

Those who claim that they have a silent religion find scant support in the Scriptures for a faith that doesn't talk.

Sacrilegious sinners may be more violent and vulgar, but our greatest problem is religious sinners.

Religious rut

Christians can get into a religious rut and fall into a mere form of godliness without power. But the true disciple is a rebel against this age because the friend of the world is the enemy of God. The Christian life is a revolution and a revolution is the opposite of a rut, which is only a grave with both ends knocked out.

Renewal

A lot of churches think they need a new preacher when they simply need the same preacher renewed. Many a preacher thinks he needs a new pastorate when he needs to be renewed in the same pastorate.

Repentance

The Great Commission is our marching orders; the last word of Christ to the church is, "Repent." To five out of seven churches in Asia it was His message. Many churches today are not ready to carry out the Great Commission until first they repent.

When a group of small boys, out to play ball, arrived at the playground, they discovered that no one had brought a ball. "Forget the ball," said one impatiently, "Let's go on with the game." We are trying to play without the ball when the church tries to evangelize before she has repented. The church can do many things after she has repented but nothing until first she repents.

The last word of our Lord to the church is not the Great Commission. The Great Commission is indeed our program to the end of the age but our Lord's last word to the church is "Repent."

We are sometimes repentant because of the harm we have done ourselves and others in our transgressions but there is little repentance toward God . . . We may regret what our sins do to our testimony and the evil effect on others but we are little concerned because the fellowship with God is broken. This makes for shallow and inadequate confession because we have not touched the heart of the trouble.

186

It takes a radical break to turn a man from earth's trash to heaven's treasure.

Repentance is almost a lost note in our preaching and experience and the lack of it is filling churches with baptized sinners who have never felt the guilt of sin or the need of a Savior.

Surely we take the goodness of God for granted. His goodness leadeth to repentance, not to complacency.

We are trying to get young people to volunteer and say, "Here am I," before they have ever said, "Woe is me!"

Reputation

A few flies can ruin a jar of precious perfume. And a little foolishness can spoil the influence of an honorable reputation.

Rest

"Come ye yourselves apart . . . and rest a while" (Mark 6:31) is a must for every Christian. If you don't come apart, you will come apart—you'll go to pieces!

I have no sympathy with those who say the devil never takes a vacation. I am not following the devil but the Lord, who said, "Come ye yourselves apart . . . and rest a while."

If we cannot go away for a vacation, we can take an "inside vacation" and find grace to help in time of need. God gives more rest than time will allow!

Some of us would do more for the Lord if we did less.

The Christian in particular and the Church in general both need to stop chopping wood long enough to whet the blade. Hours out for the Word and prayer and a week out from regular church work to revive the saints is a wise investment.

The psalmist wrote, "He that dwelleth in the secret place of the most High shall abide under the shadow of the Almighty" (Ps. 91:1). We cannot rest in God until we nest in God. To nest is to settle, to abide.

"Our eyes are upon thee." We know not what to do, but He knows. No sleeping pill can rest a man like knowing that!

The Lord Jesus knew how to rest for God, a forgotten art. Many a Christian would best glorify his Lord by a fishing trip. Maybe fishing in the creek would improve our fishing for men. We can get closer to people by getting away from them for awhile.

Results

I remember hearing Homer Hammontree, the song leader, tell when he worked with Dr. R. A. Torrey some nights would see a glorious response while others seemed to fail. But in either case Dr. Torrey simply reminded Hammontree that his responsibility was to give the message and leave the results with God.

189

Resurrection

The Emmaus disciples trudged along a lonely road in sadness. It was the third day since His crucifixion and, since it was, they should have been singing instead of sighing for He had promised to rise on that very day!

Martha believed in the resurrection, but Jesus moved her from the doctrinal to the personal: "I am the resurrection." The resurrection is not an "It" — "*I* am the resurrection." We stop too often with "It."

Revelation

The old bootblack in the barber shop was a familiar figure with his Bible always lying close at hand when he was not reading it. One day a customer said to him, "I see you're reading the Book of Revelation today. Do you understand it?" "Yes, sir, I know what it means." "You know what it means when Bible scholars have disagreed about it all these years! What do you think it means?" "It means that Jesus is gonna win!"

190

Reverence

We major nowadays on relevance and minor on reverence.

Revival

A revival is a work of God's Spirit among His own people.

The average Baptist revival runs four days, Sunday through Wednesday. There used to be a time when we took two weeks. We're not even singing "Take Time To Be Holy." We haven't got time.

We are trying to have the results of revival without the revival — the effects without the cause.

I am more afraid of a false spiritual revival than of no revival at all. We are so desperate for a visitation of God that we must beware lest we accept a synthetic substitute and for fear of attributing the work of God to the devil, wind up ascribing a work of the devil to God. The woods are full of imposters. . . .

191

Elijah was not on Carmel to demonstrate what he could do, but what God could do.

The Spirit blows where He will, and God is not bound to our grand ideas. The great Welsh revival was accomplished without preaching, without choirs, without hymn books, without organs, without publicity, and without offerings. These things are not evil, but God can do wonders without what we think He must have.

Sunday-morning Christianity is the greatest hindrance to true revival. Experience has become mere performance, "a form of godliness, but denying the power thereof . . ." (2 Tim. 3:5).

A lot of our activity often mistaken for revival is just the church turning over, but not waking up. Turning over is not getting up, and waking up is not getting up. The Word of God says we're to get up and go about our business for the King.

A revival is the church falling in love with Jesus Christ all over again. We are in love with ourselves, in love with our particular crowd, in love with our fundamentalism, maybe, but not in love with Him.

Many a so-called revival is only a drive for church members, which adds more unsaved sinners, starched and ironed but not washed, to a fellowship where even the true believers have not been aroused for years.

The Church will not get on its feet until it first gets on its knees. Ezekiel said, "The Spirit entered into me and set me upon my feet." After we have repented and are Spirit-filled, we shall stand on our feet in testimony and men shall first ask, "What meaneth this?" and then, "What shall we do?"

In that great (Welsh) revival they had no advance publicity, no choirs, no song books, no order of service or offerings, no famous preacher (great preachers attended but they sat in the congregation). All they had in this revival was God. Maybe we'll get around to that some day again. Maybe sometime heaven will come down without our "packing the pew," pin-the-tail-on-the-donkey, talking horses, karate experts, and theatrical personalities. "Where my people gather in my name, there am I . . ." — that is not just a promise but a fact!

If I were an unbeliever and dropped into the average church during a so-called revival and saw a fraction of the membership trying to get more recruits to join the army of the Lord when most of the outfit had already gone AWOL, I would surmise that Christianity is not what it is supposed to be or that we have been sold a watered-down, cheap and easy brand; that we have been inoculated with such a mild form that we are immunized against the real thing.

Everywhere we see signs advertising "Revivals." Preachers speak of "holding" revivals . . . somebody ought to turn one loose!

Riches

A man is just as rich as his investment in the bank of heaven.

Risk

There are some timid souls who never make a venture because of risks involved. Nothing ventured, nothing gained. No Columbus ever discovers a new world staying at home reading books on adventure. We have to make a plunge.

Saints

Salt

Salvation

Satan

School of Christ

Science

Scripture

Second best

Second chance

Second coming

Security

Seed

Seeking

Self

Self-condemnation

Self-deception

Self-esteem

Self-justification

Self-sufficiency

Separation

Sermons

Servants

Service

Sharing

Shepherd

Simple things

Sin

Sincerity

Singing

Sinners

Skeptics

Sleep

Smoking

Socialism

Society

Solitude

Soul

Speech

Spirit

Spirit-filled life

Spirits

Spiritual famine

Spiritual things

Stability

Statistics

Straying

Study

Stumbling blocks

Success

Sufficiency

Sunday
Christianity

Supernatural
Christian life

197

Saints

God preserves the saints, but He does not pickle them.

The tragedy of these times is that the situation is desperate but the saints are not. If the saints were as desperate as the situation something might happen. The Scriptures portray the times in terms of emergency that calls for urgency.

Many a restless saint needs not a new pasture where the grass always looks greener but a new thing done in his heart while he lives in the same pasture.

We are long on membership but short on discipleship. We are more anxious to gather statistics than to grow saints.

Salt

The outline usually runs the same course: salt seasons, purifies, preserves. But somebody ought to remind us that salt also irritates. Real living Christianity rubs this world the wrong way.

Salt preserves from spoiling and putrefaction. The world would have been utterly unendurable long ago but for the salt of the saints.

The besetting sin of our Christianity today, in private and public, is insipidity.

Salvation

Some misinterpret free salvation to involve no cost, no obligation on our part. Ours is the obligation of repentance and surrender of all we are and have.

God did not save us to make us successful but to make us holy.

God didn't save you to make you happy. That's a by-product. He saved you to make you holy. You were predestinated to be conformed to the image of God's Son.

Something used to happen to people from the outside when they became Christians. They were invaded from above. Now we try to work up something from the inside with a do-it-yourself religion.

Salvation is free. The gift of God is eternal life. It is not cheap for it cost God His Son and the Son His life, but it is free. However, when we become believers we become disciples and that will cost everything we have.

I came to Christ as a country boy. I did not understand all about the plan of salvation. One does not have to understand it, he has only to stand on it.

Surgeons and nurses must keep fit and clean, and so must we who bear the vessels of the Lord. We must keep strong; by the food of the Word, by resting in the Lord, by exercising unto godliness.

Satan

Satan, the accuser of the saints, takes great delight in worrying feeble believers who sigh when they should be singing.

Satan cannot give the Christian anything for he has everything, nor can he take away anything because he has nothing.

Satan deals in subtleties. Our Lord deals in simplicities.

Wherever there is a true work of God, I discovered that Satan employs not only opposition but imitation to defeat it. Instead of uprooting the wheat he sows tares.

Satan is clever: if he cannot lure the believer into Sodom with Lot he takes him to the other extreme and gets him into "a shew of wisdom in will-worship and humility, and neglecting of the body" which only satisfies the flesh.

Paul did not lecture on demonism in Philippi or on Artemis in Ephesus, but when his hearers became Christians they no longer practiced nor patronized evil and the devil's business was hit. When Paul won a convert the devil lost a customer.

God is the Great *I Am.* Satan is the great *I Am Not;* and he is never happier than when he has convinced people that he is non-existent. The very popular modern denial of the existence of a personal devil is one of Satan's major triumphs. We have a real enemy on our hands and we shall greatly weaken our position by blissfully disregarding his presence and power.

Satan is a great imitator and one of his devices is to simulate the work of God. Because many false prophets are gone out into the world, we need much grace and wisdom in these last days to determine if the spirits be of God. Some of them can duplicate to an amazing degree the work of God. Satan has a false gospel, a false repentance, a false dedication, a false faith, a false discipleship, a false sanctification, a false everything. Weak Christians, not well read in the Scriptures, will easily fall prey to modern magicians.

School of Christ

Our Lord said, "Learn of me," and that means studying in the school of Christ Himself. It's possible to be a magna cum laude from a college and be a first-grader in the school of Jesus Christ.

Science

Sin has gotten men into more trouble than science can get him out of.

Scripture

A businessman who was accustomed to presiding at business functions was called on suddenly to officiate at a church affair. Somebody read the Scriptures, and this man absent-mindedly got up and said, "If there are no corrections, the Scriptures will stand as read."

Second best

Are you living spiritually on crackers and cheese when you have a standing invitation daily to the banquets of His grace? The devil will lead you to get along with the good when you might have the best.

Second chance

"And the word of the Lord came unto Jonah the second time." Jonah missed his first chance, failed the Lord miserably, and suffered aplenty. But God did not disown him, he started him off again with new orders, all the wiser for a sad experience.

Second coming

The early believers were not looking for something to happen, they were looking for Someone to come. Looking for the train to arrive is one thing, but looking for someone we love to come on that train is another matter.

With regard to our Lord's return, we emphasize preparation without expectation. Of course, all too generally nothing is said of His return at all. Bringing in the Kingdom is preached, but not bringing back the King.

I'm not looking for signs. We've had plenty of them. I'm listening for a sound. Every time you see a scoffer who says there are no signs of His coming, you've just seen another sign. I'm listening for a shout.

Security

He does not always spare us trouble, but He does succor us in trouble.

Our forefathers had inner security. Ours is located in Washington, D.C.

Seed

I've seen a lot of "packaged" Christianity that sadly needs to be planted, grains of wheat that must fall into the ground and die lest they abide alone.

Seeking

When Jesus was on His way to the house of Jairus the multitude thronged Him but only one poor sick woman really touched Him (Mark 5:24-34). Multitudes throng the Lord at church on Sunday. How many really touch Him?

Self

We are always trying to "find ourselves" when that is exactly what we need to lose.

In this day of self-exaltation the Bible teaches self-execution. Not that we execute ourselves but that we submit to the death of self by the hand of God. Paul witnessed his own execution, but there came forth a new Paul: "I live, yet not I, but Christ liveth in me."

Self-condemnation

Sometimes, we want to fly before we walk; we want to be perfect before we start toward perfection. It is not a mark of godliness to be forever condemning oneself in morbid self-accusation.

Self-deception

There is one thing worse than not coming to church, and that is to come and do nothing about the message one hears. James tells us that hearing without doing means self-deception.

God wants self before substance and service.

Self-esteem

We have too few Calebs and Joshuas and too many scared spies with a grasshopper complex. The ten cowards said, ". . . we were in our own sight as grasshoppers, and so we were in their (the Canaanites) sight" (Num. 13:33). That figures. If we think we are grasshoppers, others will make it unanimous.

Self-justification

We justify ourselves when we should judge ourselves. If we learned humility, it might spare us humiliation.

Some very nice people would like to have eternal life as a good investment, but Jesus is not handing out salvation in return for another "good thing" on our self-righteous record of commandments already kept.

Self-sufficiency

Just because we have split the atom and have reached the moon, we have given God His walking papers, have decided that we can work out our own salvation and that science can answer the problem of sin.

Separation

In our well-intentioned identification with the world, we do not mold it — it molds us. We are not to be isolated but insulated, moving in the midst of evil but untouched by it.

Sermons

Illustrations in a sermon are like windows, but a sermon should not be all windows. A good story helps, but I have heard sermons that were built several stories too high!

My father's home was the staying place for the preachers in the horse and buggy days. We had only one sermon a month — some of them were long enough to last a month.

An old minister explained the blurs on his sermon outlines by saying they were caused by sweat and tears. And without those two marks, a sermon is not a sermon.

The man on the street never heard of existentialism, for instance, and couldn't care less. It's about time we quit answering questions nobody is asking and spoke to the plain needs of human hearts.

Does your message end with one point like a sword or does it end like a broom with a thousand straws?

Some preachers ought to put more fire into their sermons or more sermons into the fire.

There is a world of difference between a sermon on your mind and a sermon on your heart — between getting things off your chest and pouring out your heart — between carrying your church on your back and carrying it in your heart.

There is only one way to turn sermons from weights to wings. When the man in the pulpit rises to that lofty realm where he is fired with a sense of mission, when he has a burning in his bones, a word from God to give to men regardless of how they receive it, then he is set free from his shackles.

Servants

Some little boys were playing war. When an on-looker asked why they were so quiet, one boy replied, "We're all generals, we can't get anybody to do the fighting!"

Service

Our Lord holds the keys to the doors of Christian service. You don't have to chase "key men" around if you know the Keeper of the Keys!

The average church member would do well to look in his concordance and see how many columns it takes to list all the "serve," "servant," "service" references. We come to church to sit but will not go out to serve.

The Philippian jailer cared nothing about the sufferings of Paul and Silas until he knew Christ, then he washed the stripes of his prisoners.

Sharing

We are not salt cellars but saltshakers to scatter our blessings everywhere we go.

Shepherd

The shepherd went after the sheep. Nowadays we have built comfortable folds and have put on the outside: "Any lost sheep reporting here will be taken care of."

Simple things

The Savior talked about simple things like salt and bread and water and His parables have endured while symposiums where scholars pool their ignorance have been forgotten.

Sin

We still carry the marks of Adam's fall, and our bifocals and bridges and baldness and all our frailties bear witness that we are his offspring.

Little by little sin is made to appear less sinful. We are being homogenized, absorbed, assimilated into this age. We accept its literature, its music, its art, its language, without inner or outer protest although we are told to hate evil, abhor evil, abstain from the very appearance of evil.

There was a time when sin shocked some of you that it's not shocking now. I heard Lucille Ball say one time, "I'm shocked that I'm not shocked anymore."

It is not the Word hidden in the head but in the heart that keeps us from sin.

He came to save us, not from poverty or from ignorance or from the ghetto, but from our sins. Sin must be dealt with first.

We must deal with the seeds of sin in our hearts. If neglected the seeds soon become weeds. Let us deal with the seeds and we shall have no trouble with the weeds.

We do not have healthy hatred of sin today because we have no proper sense of the holiness of God. The love of God has been preached but not His law. Men are not conscious of their need because they do not regard sin as the awful thing that cost God His Son and the Son His life. They do not desire the Physician because they do not think they are sick.

People used to blush when they were ashamed. Now they are ashamed if they blush. Modesty has disappeared and a brazen generation with no fear of God before its eyes mocks at sin. We are so fond of being called tolerant and broadminded that we wink at sin when we ought to weep.

214

Sin is moral leprosy. To put up with leprosy is to die of leprosy. Sin is spiritual cancer. A man who tries only to live with cancer, dies with it. If we do not deal with spiritual malignancy, then indeed it deals with us.

There was a time when sin shocked us. But as the brainwashing progresses, what once amazed us only amuses us. We laugh at the shady joke; tragedy becomes comedy; we learn to speak the language of Vanity Fair.

Sincerity

When people do not mean business with Christ in their hearts they will not do business for Christ with their hands.

There is no place in Scripture for the type of church member who sings, "O How I Love Jesus," but feeds no sheep; who sings, "Rescue the Perishing," but does no rescue work himself.

Singing

Some saints spend more time sighing than singing!

One sure mark of revival is, it sets people singing. When showers of blessing fall, the congregation begins to sing. God is not only salvation, He is our song and He puts a new song in our mouths, even praise unto Him. Saving grace is singing grace and if we are not singing, at least in our hearts, we had better check on our state. Beware of a Christian profession that is words without music, mandates without melody. Your salvation, standing and service should be accompanied by a song.

The psalmist indicates that we are strangers and pilgrims in this world and while we make our way through it we have a song. That song is God's Word itself. The writer did not just memorize it or quote it, he sang it.

Sinners

Men do not see themselves as sinners, so they do not grow sick of sin nor forsake it; they join our churches on empty professions of faith, carrying their sins with them.

216

My preacher friend, don't stomp on sinners when you go out to preach. My Lord didn't come to condemn the world, but that the world through Him might be saved. Bless God, He didn't come down here to rub it in; He came to rub it out. Tell them that.

Skeptics

Too many are not willing to give the Gospel a fair trial. They are too ignorant to speak wisely but not wise enough to speak ignorantly. A man is not a sinner because he is a skeptic; he is a skeptic because he is a sinner.

Sleep

I think of the old bishop who could not sleep, so at two in the morning he got up and started reading his Bible. He came to where it says, "He that keepeth Israel neither slumbers nor sleeps." He said, "Well, Lord, if You're sitting up, I'm going to bed. Good night."

Smoking

I'm tired of wading through secondhand tobacco smoke from a generation of lung cancer prospects. I hear about "I'd rather fight than switch," but what bothers me is this crowd that would rather die than quit.

Socialism

My father would never have gone out for the new so-called Christian Socialism that tries to rehabilitate the prodigal before he has returned to the father's house. He was not for building bigger and better hogpens in the Far Country. He believed you needed a new heart first, then came the robe and ring and the fatted calf. He didn't read in his New Testament that the prodigal said, "I will arise and apply for government relief."

Society

I was in a motel the other day that had a little notice up just for fun, but it had a point. It said, "We will now accept dogs. We have not admitted dogs, but we can have dogs stay here now." It said, "After all, no dog ever set the place on fire with a cigarette. No dog ever went out without paying his bill. No dog ever stole our blankets." Then it had a little notice down underneath that was for us folks: "If you can get your dog to vouch for you, we'll let you stay here too." We are in a bad way when we have to get the endorsement of a dog to stay somewhere.

There's a right way to identify with society and a wrong way. Our Lord told us what this is in John 17:18 and once and for all located us in this world. We've been saved out of it to go right back into it to win other people out of it, and that's the only business we have in it.

Solitude

Solitary meditation is a lost art. Americans cannot endure their own company. What could be worse for the average American than a rainy afternoon with TV out of order!

Soul

God does not give the soul a vacation, He gives it a vocation.

Speech

The Bible has a lot to say about our mouths, our lips, our tongues, for our speech betrays us. What is down in the well will come up in the bucket.

The old country doctor of my boyhood days always began his examination by saying, "Let me see your tongue." It is a good way to start the examination of anybody. "Whoso keepeth his mouth and his tongue keepth his soul from troubles" (Prov. 21:23).

Spirit

Avoid the cumbered spirit. The church at Sardis was busy with a lot of good things but did not get through to God with them. There was too much Martha, not enough Mary. How easy to be "cumbered with a load of care," even about good things! We can work in a bakery and lose our taste for bread.

220

To be "fervent in spirit" is to be "boiling in spirit," and to boil we must be near the Fire.

A Christian is filled with the Spirit when he realizes his need, puts away all known sin, surrenders to Christ all he is and has, and by faith receives the fulness of the Spirit that he may glorify Jesus Christ in his life and testimony.

Much of our Christianity today is like the feast at Cana. . . . We have a feast of good things: there is plenty of teaching and preaching; churches and conferences spread tables loaded with superabundance. But we have no wine. The exhilaration of the spirit is lacking.

Our world is drunk. Some Christians are drunk on false wine, having fired themselves with the energy of the flesh. It will take the true wine of the Spirit to move this world.

It is not what is done for God that counts, but rather what is done by Him, the work of His Spirit through our yielded wills.

Spirit-filled life

The heart is deceitful and one may well ask, "Why do I wish to be Spirit-filled?" We may think we seek only to glorify God and help others when underneath there lurks the sneaking ambition to be possessed of something that will set us apart in an exclusive category for others to watch and admire. If that is the case, then we have neither part nor lot in this matter, as Peter said, for our hearts are not right in the sight of God.

Spirits

No gift of God is scarcer and at the same time more necessary than the discerning of spirits. The natural man knows nothing about it. The carnal man is devoid of it. Only the spiritual man can have it.

Spiritual famine

There is spiritual famine today and some well-meaning church leaders are trying to alleviate the drought by social reforms and government projects under church auspices.

Spiritual things

One might as well talk nuclear physics to a wooden Indian in front of a cigar store as to discuss spiritual things to a natural man.

One might as well describe a sunset to a blind man or music to a deaf man as to talk about the deep things of God to a man who has never been born again.

Stability

The true Christian has living, not dead, stability. He is not like a tombstone but like a tree planted by the rivers of water.

Statistics

We were predestinated to be conformed to the image of God's Son. What shall we say of multitudes of church members who are no more like Jesus today than they were twenty-five years ago? God intended that we be more than statistics. He would have us be saints.

He is a successful minister or physician who re-members that his parishioners or patients are not statistics on a church roll or appointments on a calendar but people with the same basic needs today that they have had since Adam.

Straying

We take a detour as motorists because we have to. As Christians we take it because we want to. But, thank God, Abraham and Jacob and Jonah and Peter did not die on the detour. And if you are a "detourist" the Lord is looking for you.

Study

It is tragic to go through our days making Christ the subject of our study but not the sustenance of our souls. To appropriate Christ Himself, the Bread of Life, is to live by faith and grow. You can starve reading books on bread.

Stumbling blocks

Paul turned his stumbling-blocks into stepping-stones. John Bunyan in Bedford jail, Fanny Crosby in a prison of blindness "out of weakness were made strong." Long is the list of saints through the ages who have turned minus to plus by the grace of God.

Success

Visible success has never been the proof of Jesus or His followers.

He who tries to use this world's textbooks on success in the things of the Spirit will end up like the man who offered to sell a set of books on "How to Succeed" for a month's room and board! It just doesn't work.

Many a prophet has been promoted into silence. Success can feather our nest so comfortably that we forget how to fly. Abraham's servant, when tempted to stay awhile at the home of the wife he had found for Isaac, said, "Hinder me not, seeing the Lord hath prospered my way . . ." If God has prospered your way, you had better be on your way!

Sufficiency

Our efficiency turns out to be a deficiency unless we have His sufficiency.

God abounds and we abound. There will always be enough of all we need to do all that God wants us to do as long as He wants us to do it.

Sunday Christianity

The Lord's Day crowd does not delight me; it depresses me because it indicates a Sunday morning Christianity that is the greatest hindrance to real revival. It pays God a tribute of one hour at church and then says "Goodbye, God, I'll see you next Sunday." These Sunday morning glories, who bloom only to fold up for the rest of the week, are often a greater problem than the publicans and sinners outside the church.

Supernatural Christian life

The Christian life itself is a miracle and every phase of it ought to bear the mark of the supernatural.

God won't do the supernatural thing until we do the simple thing. We try to do what only God can do, and we don't do what we must do.

Technology

Many of the distempers of society are the sad consequence of no longer being able to walk and think. Man's gadgetry has made him its slave and prisoner. Gaining the world of technology we have paid for it—with our souls.

Temptation

He does not keep us from temptation, but He can keep us in temptation.

Terminology

They tell us we need a new lingo today. We must learn the new terminology. Instead of a problem, it's a "hang-up." Instead of a blessing, it's a "meaningful experience." What difference does it make what they call it? They used to call it "itch" and now it's "allergy," but you scratch just the same.

Testing

When we go through God's testing properly, all we lose are the shackles that tied us up earlier — we have been set free!

Thankfulness

Our biggest problem in the church today is this vast majority of Sunday morning Christians who claim to have known the Master's cure and who return not on Sunday night or Wednesday night or during revivals to thank Him by presence, prayer, testimony and support of His church. In fact, the whole Christian life is one big "Thank You," the living expression of our gratitude to God for His goodness. But we take Him for granted and what we take for granted we never take seriously.

Time

If our lives and ministry count for anything today, we must solemnly resolve to make time for God.

A South Carolina friend told me about meeting a typical old Southern gentleman who said, "I used to come over to your town quite often in the old days. It was a day's round trip by horse and buggy. I can do it now in an hour but I don't have time!" That just about sums up the tempo and the tragedy of these hurried times.

We ought to watch and pray because of the short-
ness of the time, the seriousness of the hour, and
the shallowness of our nature.

Tobacco

The devil advertises tobacco not with lung cancer
victims, but with attractive girls.

I never preach about tobacco. I just tell my crowd
to leave its tobacco outside and I'll guarantee that
no hog or dog will bother it.

Translations of the Bible

There is some help in new translations, but it is
remarkable how much treasure some of our fathers dug out of the old King James.

Trends

Trendism is the order of the day, and we are a generation of Trendists. The man of God was never meant to catch the spirit of the times, but to condemn and correct it.

Tribulation

The right side is not always the bright side immediately, but it will be ultimately. "In the world ye shall have tribulation"—that is the dark side. "But be of good cheer; I have overcome the world"—that is the bright side.

All the tribulations of this life are but incidents on the road from Groans to Glory.

Trivia

It is possible to be submerged and overcome by trivial matters not that important. It is no disgrace to be the victim of a lion but there is no excuse for allowing ourselves to be bitten to death by mosquitoes.

Letting trivial troubles get us down is poor preparation for real adversity. Some of us frazzle ourselves battling mosquitoes and are exhausted when we face the lion. Each victory will help us another to win and we do well to practice on the minors to get ready for the majors.

Trust

Looking back to the good old days is not the way out. Looking up to the God of ALL the Days is.

The highest lesson God wants to teach us is to "trust Him regardless." If everything made sense to our understanding we would need no faith.

Jesus does not say, "There is no storm." He says, "I am here, do not toss but trust."

Tuned-in

Are you tuned in on God? It is said that John Burroughs, the naturalist, could walk along a noisy street and overhear a cricket in the hedge. His ear was tuned to the little voices of nature. You can make your way through the hubbub and still keep in touch with heaven.

Unity

Urgency

Unity

We are busy these days with union and unification trying to get the saints together, but what is needed is unity, and that we find only in heart-fellowship with Jesus Christ.

Urgency

There is little sense of emergency and therefore little sense of urgency. If we realize that we are Last-minute Men, that the time is short, we shall be Minute Men, ready at a moment's notice.

Vacation

Vengeance

Vision

Vitamins

Vacation

We should learn to take an "inside" vacation, within ourselves. Merely taking an "outside" vacation, changing the scenery, will do no good if the same old inner strain goes along. "Getting away from it all" is usually a great delusion, for we generally take it all with us.

Vengeance

"I'll give her a piece of my mind" is often the first salvo in a bitter verbal war. Giving away pieces of our minds is poor business. We can't afford it, for one thing, because we do not have that much mind to spare! And we would have more peace of mind if we gave away fewer pieces of our minds. If we are the Lord's, the battle is His and vengeance is His. "Say not thou, I will recompense evil; but wait on the Lord, and he shall save thee" (Prov. 20:22).

Vision

The vision must be followed by the venture. It is not enough to stare up the steps—we must step up the stairs.

Vitamins

He is the Bread of Life. All the vitamins and calories your soul requires are in Christ. He is Alpha and Omega—and all the letters between.

240

Walking

War

Wastefulness

Wholeness

Wisdom

Witnesses

Witnessing

Women

Wonder

Wonderful

Word of God

Work

World

World view

Worldlines

Worry

Worship

Walking

Walking is a lost art. Any pedestrian along a country road these days is presumed to be either out of his head or out of gas.

God ordained walking, the perfect exercise; but walking is still an un-American activity. If you see somebody strolling along a highway actually thinking, you pronounce him out of his head or out of gas.

War

How many today live with war in their hearts because that which is of the flesh contends with that which is of faith! Call it inhibitions, complexes, neuroses, dress it up in psychiatric verbiage, it is but Ishmael and Isaac warring in the soul.

Wastefulness

This is an age of unprecedented wastefulness. We are prodigal in our utter misuse of time, energy, ability, our bodies, minds and souls. We squander the treasures of time and talent, burning the candle at both ends, a generation of spendthrifts.

Wholeness

We are complete in Him, not in any experience or favorite doctrine. The whole is greater than any of the parts.

Wisdom

If you lack knowledge, go to school. If you lack wisdom, get on your knees! Knowledge is not wisdom. Wisdom is proper use of knowledge.

Witnesses

Jesus takes the disciple and makes not a depository but a dispenser out of him and through him reaches others.

Churchill said of England's airmen in World War II, "Never did so many owe so much to so few." Of God's remnant of witnesses today we may say, "Never did so few owe so much to so many!"

Witnessing

Before our gospelizing gets around to the uttermost part of the earth, it should begin at home, "in Jerusalem" as it were. We have a story to tell to the nations, but it is also a story to tell to the neighbors all around us.

There is too much sermonizing and too little witnessing. People do not come to Christ at the end of an argument. Simon Peter comes to Jesus because Andrew goes after him with a testimony.

I know that some are always studying the meaning of the fourth toe of the right foot of some beast in prophecy and have never used either foot to go and bring men to Christ. I do not know who the 666 is in Revelation but I know this world is sick, sick, sick, and the best way to speed the Lord's return is to win more souls for Him.

It takes a Person to reach persons, a Life to reach lives. The Gospel is a personal matter: "HE shall save His people from THEIR sins." "If I be lifted up I will draw all men unto ME."

No translation is quite as effective as the flesh-and-blood edition. Alas, some of these are very incomplete and some are parodies of the text. Some are private revisions, not translations, of the original. Remember, a world is watching us. May our translations be true in letter and spirit.

If we are ever going to be or do or say anything for our Lord, now is the time.

In Boston I saw a plaque marking the spot where an obscure Christian laid a hand on a broad-shouldered New Englander and so brought Dwight L. Moody to know Christ. That bit of bread cast upon the waters has traveled around the world and is still washing up in blessing on the shores of every continent.

When anything good comes our way we usually tell it. Strange that the greatest good tidings of all should find us holding our peace. Maybe we have just become canvassers looking for "members" instead of gatherers looking for souls.

Women

Let it be said to the credit of womanhood that there is no record in the Gospel of any woman ever opposing Jesus.

Wonder

Oldsters have no time to wonder, to reflect, to meditate about anything. We must always be "doing something." There is no time to walk in the woods, to sit before an open fire, "just thinking." Everything is organized, supervised, planned, programmed, and correlated. We don't walk, we take organized hikes. We don't wander along, watching birds, we join a club and keep records. We lose the wonder of it in the work of it.

Wonderful

A passenger on a long train trip was so enthralled by the journey that every few moments he was heard to say, "Wonderful!" The passing scenery, the faces of the fellow passengers, even the smallest details elicited from him glad expressions of keen enjoyment. Finally one traveler, overcome by curiosity, asked him, "How is it that while the rest of us are worn out with this monotonous trip, you are having the time of your life?" He answered, "Until a few days ago, I was a blind man. A great doctor has just given me my sight and what is ordinary to the rest of you is out of this world to me."

Word of God

Sometimes the airplane pilot can see nothing and must fly by instrument. The Christian must often do the same and that instrument is the Word of God. It guarantees a safe landing!

In a day of tranquilizers we are likely to make an aspirin pill of religion. The Word of God is not a lullaby to put us to sleep but a reveille to wake us up.

Work

I came to the conclusion that God is not interested in mere quantity production and that we sometimes can do more by doing less.

It is true that the devil never takes a vacation, but we are not to follow the devil but the Lord. Jesus was never in a hurry, and we need to learn the gait of Galilee.

Idleness is the devil's workshop, but so is busyness if, while we are busy here and there, we fail in our main responsibility. "And as thy servant was busy here and there, he was gone . . ." (1 Kings 20:40).

World

Today the world has so infiltrated the church that we are more beset by traitors within than by foes without. Satan is not fighting churches, he is joining them. He does more harm by sowing tares than by pulling up the wheat. He accomplishes more by imitation than by outright opposition. The world is accepted into the church and its programs endorsed. Worldly celebrities are called in to enhance the gospel and preachers participate in the performances of the ungodly. The same popular singer combines sensuous publicity in the papers with the gospel songs in the record shops. Preachers make clowns of themselves and churches become theaters.

The Christian faith is not a way to explain, enjoy, or endure this world but to overcome it.

World view

It is debatable which is causing us more harm — hot-headed ignorance or cold-hearted intellectualism.

The tragedy of today is that the situation is desperate but the saints are not.

Worldliness

Worldliness is rampant in the church. The devil is not fighting churches, he is joining them! He isn't persecuting Christianity, he is professing it.

Worry

It is not work but worry that kills, and it is amazing how much wear the human mind and body can stand if it is free from friction and well oiled by the Spirit. A mind at leisure from itself beats all the rest cures.

Worship

Our Lord approved neither idol worship or idle worship but ideal worship in Spirit and truth.

Too many church services start at eleven o'clock sharp and end at twelve o'clock dull.

Too many church members sit smugly in church on Sunday, some closing the eyes and others eyeing the clothes, and with a dozen other things ahead of God in their lives.

Everybody comes on Sunday morning, but the middle of the week shows who is who. Nowadays when what used to be the Lord's Day has become the weekend, and the holy day is now a holiday, we may have to make more than we ever did of the midweek service.

Youth

Youth

Young people often talk with me about their struggle with whether to preach or not to preach. I tell them if they think they feel led to preach, give God the benefit of the doubt and preach. God will bless you in spite of yourself.

We commonly think that life's major decisions are made by older people, but, actually, the three greatest choices anyone can make are usually decided on by young people before they reach their middle twenties. The salvation of the soul, the choice of a life work and a life companion, these are life's greatest decisions, and young people make them.

Youth today is asking, "Who am I?" but few are willing to face what they really are: sinners separated from God. Too many sermons addressed to young people congratulate and compliment them and cater to their pride and rebellion until they are in no mood to repent.